YOUTH

and the

WRITINGS OF NICHIREN DAISHONIN

YOUTH

and the

WRITINGS OF NICHIREN DAISHONIN

SGI PRESIDENT IKEDA'S LECTURE SERIES

World Tribune
Press

Published by WORLD TRIBUNE PRESS
606 Wilshire Blvd.
Santa Monica, CA 90401

Printed in the United States of America.

Design by *the*BookDesigners
Cover design by Gopa & Ted2, Inc.

ISBN: 978-1-935523-38-3

10 9 8 7 6 5 4 3 2 1

Contents

——— Introduction ———

The discussions in this book took place among Soka Gakkai youth leaders and SGI President Ikeda and published as a youth study series based on *The Writings of Nichiren Daishonin*. The series began in the January 25, 2010, *Seikyo Shimbun* (the Soka Gakkai's daily newspaper) and ended in the December 29, 2010, *Seikyo Shimbun*. These installments were later published in the *World Tribune,* from the February 26, 2010, issue to the November 18, 2011, issue.

Editor's Note

- GZ, page number(s)—refers to the *Gosho zenshu*, the Japanese-language compilation of letters, treatises, essays and oral teachings of Nichiren Daishonin.

- LSOC, page number(s)—refers to *The Lotus Sutra and Its Opening and Closing Sutras*, translated by Burton Watson (Tokyo: Soka Gakkai, 2009).

- OTT, page number(s)—refers to *The Record of the Orally Transmitted Teachings*, translated by Burton Watson (Soka Gakkai: Tokyo, 2004).

- WND, page number(s)—refers to *The Writings of Nichiren Daishonin*, vol. 1 (WND-1) (Tokyo: Soka Gakkai, 1999) and vol. 2 (WND-2) (Tokyo: Soka Gakkai, 2006).

———— One ————

Chanting With the Shared Vow of Mentor and Disciple

SGI President Daisaku Ikeda: We are living in an age of dynamic change, an age that calls for the active participation of youth. Young people possess courage, vitality and vision. The time has come for youth to step up and shoulder full responsibility for our epic movement of worldwide kosen-rufu. That is why I would like to take this opportunity to talk with you, our young men and women, who have such an important mission, and discuss the essential points for living a victorious youth, based on the writings of Nichiren Daishonin.

Soka Gakkai Youth Division Leader Yoshinori Sato: President Ikeda, as representatives of the youth division, we deeply appreciate your giving us this opportunity to study with you. We are determined to strive and win by applying ourselves energetically to the two ways of practice and study, and live up to your aspirations for us.

Soka Gakkai Young Women's Division Leader Yumiko Kumazawa: Under your guidance and instruction, we have the chance to learn and practice the world's foremost life philosophy. We are truly fortunate to lead such a fulfilling and meaningful youth. But there are so many other young people who lack a clear sense of purpose and direction in life. We are now even more strongly committed to sharing the philosophy of Nichiren Buddhism with them.

President Ikeda: That's wonderful to hear.

I'm counting on all of you to do your best. A grand and unparalleled stage for your youthful endeavors lies open before you. If you don't joyfully dance out onto this brilliant stage, you will only be shortchanging yourselves.

Nichiren says: "Great joy [is what] one experiences when one understands for the first time that one's mind from the very beginning has been the Buddha. [Chanting] Nam-myoho-renge-kyo is the greatest of all joys" (see OTT, 211–12).

Your lives are more precious and noble than you can even imagine. They are storehouses of infinite treasures. With courageous faith, you can tap more and more of your inner potential and allow it to shine forth brilliantly.

Mr. Sato: Thank you for your faith in us.

Most of the news on television or in the papers is dark and depressing, leaving a lot of young people feeling hopeless and disillusioned. We of the youth division, on the other hand, thanks to your constant encouragement to us as our mentor in life, are able to advance with a powerful sense of hope, no matter what. We will share this worthy path with as many other youth as possible and expand our network of like-minded people.

President Ikeda: The Daishonin states unequivocally, "If the Law that one embraces is supreme, then the person who embraces it must accordingly be foremost among all others" (WND-1, 61). A person can be measured by the philosophy they embrace and practice.

All of you have the good fortune to be practicing the world's supreme philosophy in your youth, and you are making positive contributions to society. This makes you people of unsurpassed nobility. Always live with that sense of pride.

Ms. Kumazawa: Yes, we always will.

The American futurist Hazel Henderson once said to a group of our young women's student division members, "I think that one of the great things that the Soka Gakkai gives to you all is an understanding of your own potential and the desire to give to the world—because this is the way we are fulfilled and the way to happiness."[1]

We are leading the most meaningful youth and winning the praise of many thinking people around the globe.

Answering the Fundamental Questions of Life and Death

President Ikeda: People the world over are thirsting for a truly humanistic philosophy, a philosophy of respect for the dignity of life. When I was young, I always carried *The Writings of Nichiren Daishonin* with me wherever I went. I read it every chance I had, including when I was riding the train to visit different regions.

Mr. Sato: I heard of a woman who took a seat with her young daughter opposite to you on the train toward the end of 1957. She decided to start practicing Nichiren Buddhism because of the warm encouragement you gave her during that brief encounter. Speaking of that time many years later, she said she clearly remembered you being engrossed in a thick book bound in black leather.

Ms. Kumazawa: It was *The Writings of Nichiren Daishonin*, wasn't it?

President Ikeda: Yes. Well, I didn't dare show my face to second Soka Gakkai president Josei Toda if I hadn't studied *The Writings of Nichiren Daishonin*. I was in earnest because I knew that without really studying the Daishonin's writings, I couldn't deepen my own faith or encourage many members.

One winter day when I went to see Mr. Toda, he looked very tired. Even so, he said to me, "Feel free to ask me any questions you have." I felt bad about troubling him when he seemed so exhausted, but when I asked him about the "Hyaku rokka sho" ("The One Hundred and Six Comparisons," GZ, 854–69), which I was studying at the time, he smiled and gave me a very profound lesson on this writing. I'll never forget that. He always responded with tremendous enthusiasm to the sincere seeking spirit of youth.

Ms. Kumazawa: The SGI Ikeda Kayo-kai members are intently studying your lectures on Nichiren's writings, just as if you were addressing them personally. [President Ikeda established the international young women's training group in September 2008.]

President Ikeda: We are so fortunate to have *The Writings of Nichiren Daishonin*. It is an incredible source of strength. The Daishonin teaches us that nothing surpasses the strategy of the Lotus Sutra, that is, chanting Nam-myoho-renge-kyo.

Strive to read even a passage or a page of *The Writings of Nichiren Daishonin*. I hope you will always seek to understand and learn from Nichiren's spirit.

Mr. Toda used to say, "If you feel deadlocked, open *The Writings of Nichiren Daishonin*" and "When you're exhausted, that's the time to engrave the Daishonin's writings in your heart."

When we open and read *The Writings of Nichiren Daishonin*, it can bring boundless hope, courage and wisdom to well forth from within us, filling us with unshakable conviction. *The Writings of Nichiren Daishonin* is like an inexhaustible spring.

Ms. Kumazawa: A women's division leader who spoke at one of our young women's gatherings once said: "The answers to all of life's problems can be found in *The Writings of Nichiren Daishonin*. As the Daishonin reminds us, 'Winter always turns to spring' (WND-1, 536)."

President Ikeda: That's right. Without Nichiren Buddhism, it is beyond the means of even the most brilliant scholar or most powerful billionaire to find a way of solving the fundamental problems of the human condition—[the "four sufferings"] birth, aging, sickness and death.

The Daishonin calmly states, "The varied sufferings that all living beings undergo—all these are Nichiren's own sufferings" (OTT, 138). And in *The Writings of Nichiren Daishonin*, he sets forth the answer to how we can triumph over all sufferings without fail.

Our members in Japan and around the world have demonstrated this incomparable power to overcome life's hardships, their lives brimming with the "four virtues" of eternity, happiness, true self and purity. They are dedicating themselves to spreading the humanistic teachings and principles of Buddhism for the sake of the peace and prosperity of their countries and communities, in accord with Nichiren's tenet of "establishing the correct teaching for the peace of the land." This has been the proud history of the Soka Gakkai over the past eighty years.

Prayer Is the Driving Force for Everything

Mr. Sato: We of the youth division are determined to carry on the Soka Gakkai spirit and open a new, triumphant page of history in the annals of our movement. Therefore, for our first session today, would it be possible for you to talk about prayer, or chanting Nam-myoho-renge-kyo, which is the driving force for all our efforts?

Ms. Kumazawa: President Ikeda, we have recently been very fortunate to chant together with you at the headquarters leaders meetings and at the rebroadcasts of those gatherings. Many members have expressed their appreciation and renewed determination, saying that it has deeply invigorated and inspired them in faith.

President Ikeda: Chanting Nam-myoho-renge-kyo is the driving force for everything. I often chanted together with Mr. Toda. Each of those occasions was very precious—whether it was at the Soka Gakkai Headquarters, at his home or at some meeting place on our travels throughout Japan together.

Once, right at the height of Mr. Toda's business crisis, he said to me strictly, "You can't make an all-out effort if your life force is weak." He then chanted with me.

In *The Record of the Orally Transmitted Teachings*, the Daishonin defines the meaning of the term *lion's roar*, "The 'roar' is the sound of the teacher and the disciples chanting in unison" (OTT, 111).[2] Chanting together with Mr. Toda created a lion's roar powerful enough to shake the entire universe. It resounded with a dauntless assurance of victory.

Prayer is the heart of religion. It is a sublime act distinct to human beings.

Our attitude is clearly reflected in our chanting—in what we are chanting for and how earnestly or seriously we are chanting. Chanting to the Gohonzon is a profound ceremony of communion between the individual microcosm of our lives and the macrocosm of the universe as a whole. This is because Nam-myoho-renge-kyo is the fundamental law that governs our lives and the universe.

Mr. Sato: This is completely different from the stance of expecting some sort of external supernatural being to bestow blessings on us.

President Ikeda: Yes. It's not a matter of simply worshipping something to have your wishes granted. "Buddhism is reason" (WND-1, 839), Nichiren writes.

I have also said this to the sports division members, but true prayer in Nichiren Buddhism leads directly to making all-out efforts.

Buddhism teaches that human life is immeasurably precious and respecworthy. Chanting Nam-myoho-renge-kyo is the Buddhist practice that actualizes life's limitless potential. Indeed, chanting Nam-myoho-renge-kyo has unlimited power to unlock the latent positive potential of all humankind.

Ms. Kumazawa: New members often want to know what is the correct way for them to chant.

President Ikeda: There's no need to overcomplicate things. You just need to sit in front of the Gohonzon as you are, and then chant honestly and naturally about whatever is troubling you or causing you suffering. As the Daishonin says: "Suffer what there is to suffer, enjoy what there is to enjoy. Regard both suffering and joy as facts of life, and continue chanting Nam-myoho-renge-kyo, no matter what happens" (WND-1, 681).

Mr. Sato: All around Japan, members who have recently started practicing are experiencing the great benefit of faith and deepening their conviction.

President Ikeda: That's wonderful. In "The True Aspect of All Phenomena," Nichiren writes, "Were they not Bodhisattvas of the Earth, they could not chant the daimoku" (WND-1, 385). Being able to chant attests to a profound karmic connection with this Buddhism. And as the Daishonin also notes, "If you are of the same mind as Nichiren, you must be a Bodhisattva of the Earth" (WND-1, 385). All of you, young men and women who are chanting Nam-myoho-renge-kyo and dedicating your lives to kosen-rufu, are infinitely respectworthy Bodhisattvas of the Earth.

Mr. Sato: So that means that the *daimoku* we chant with a commitment to work for kosen-rufu, as members of the SGI, is daimoku that is based on the vow of Bodhisattvas of the Earth.

I recall your sharing these words from President Toda with us: "Chant daimoku infused with genuine resolve! Daimoku is a sharp sword, a jeweled saber. You must win with daimoku!"

President Ikeda: You are chanting Nam-myoho-renge-kyo for others' happiness and the realization of kosen-rufu. You are engaging in SGI activities and making efforts to share the teachings of Nichiren Buddhism with others. As such, your prayers and actions are indicative of a profound vow or commitment.

In "Emerging from the Earth," the 15th chapter of the Lotus Sutra, the Bodhisattvas of the Earth appear from the ground and vow to carry out kosen-rufu—or the widespread propagation of the correct teaching—in the Latter Day of the Law. It is in accord with that vow that we have been born into this world at this time and are striving to realize the lofty goal of kosen-rufu as members of the SGI. Some of you might say, "Hey, wait a minute, I don't remember making any such vow!" But viewed from the perspective of Buddhism and the law of cause and effect operating in our lives, it is the solemn reality.

Mr. Sato: In modern times, it has been none other than the successive presidents of the Soka Gakkai and their disciples in Japan and throughout the world who have striven to actualize this vow of the Bodhisattvas of the Earth.

President Ikeda: The other day, we were finally able to make contact with our members in Haiti, following the devastating earthquake that took place there (on January 12, 2010). The destruction has been staggering in its scope. I'd like to offer my sincerest condolences to all those affected by the disaster, and I am praying fervently for the country to make the speediest possible recovery.

In a report he sent to us in the aftermath of that catastrophic event, SGI-Haiti Chapter Leader Niaud Pierre wrote: "We have the Gohonzon, we have President Ikeda, and we have our noble friends of the SGI. We have the courage to move forward despite all. Sensei, the members of Haiti will keep winning, no matter what!"

SGI-Haiti will hold its first post-earthquake discussion meeting (on January 24, 2010). It has received warm support from members of the neighboring Dominican Republic, who have traveled to Haiti to help with the relief effort.

As members of the SGI, we are all deeply and solidly connected by our dedicated prayers infused with a vow for kosen-rufu. The SGI is an organization that is carrying out the Buddha's decree—an organization powered by our awareness that we are Bodhisattvas of the Earth. Its mission is truly noble and profound. Without our conviction in being Bodhisattvas of the Earth, we would not be able to overcome the "three powerful enemies" and actualize kosen-rufu in the evil age of the Latter Day of the Law.

Ms. Kumazawa: The first three presidents of the Soka Gakkai—founding president Tsunesaburo Makiguchi, second president Josei Toda and you, President Ikeda—are the ones who have personally taught us what it means to lead a life dedicated to the vow for kosen-rufu.

Nichiren's Writings Offer Profound Insights Into Our Lives

President Ikeda: Mr. Toda declared, "All of us who are striving for kosen-rufu were present at the Ceremony in the Air of the Lotus Sutra."

In other words, we tell others about Buddhism and work for kosen-rufu not because someone else has told us to; we have all actually been born as Bodhisattvas of the Earth as a result of our own wish and vow from the past. When we read Nichiren Daishonin's writings with that conviction, his words will resonate in our lives that much more deeply and meaningfully. The same is true of the Lotus Sutra. As the Daishonin writes, "The storehouse of the eighty-four thousand teachings [of the Buddha] represents a day-to-day record of one's own existence" (WND-2, 843).

The SGI is strong and invincible because we study the writings of Nichiren Daishonin as teachings that offer profound insight into our lives.

Ms. Kumazawa: The Bodhisattvas of the Earth break through the thick crust of the earth and emerge dancing joyously. Likewise, we, the young women's division members, are determined to live out our lives in an upbeat, positive spirit, dedicated to our own unique missions, without being defeated by the various problems we encounter.

President Ikeda: Yes. The Bodhisattvas of the Earth always willingly emerge at the most challenging times and places. That is the case for all of us in the SGI.

The problems you may currently be facing are, from the perspective of Buddhism, part of your own chosen mission. Forging ahead with that conviction is proof that your chanting is infused with a vow for kosen-rufu.

Chanting earnestly is the way to triumph over the various problems that assail us, whether they be related to work, finances, human relations, illness and so on. And our showing actual proof of victory by overcoming our problems can serve as a source of hope and inspiration for others facing similar challenges.

We can transform karma into mission through chanting Nam-myoho-renge-kyo with the recognition that we have voluntarily assumed the appropriate karma in order to show the power of the Mystic Law to others in this lifetime. It is crucial that we summon forth our courage, and chant for the happiness of ourselves and others. This is an expression of deep compassion. By chanting not only for our own happiness but that of others, as well, we can attain a lofty and expansive state of life that allows us to be undaunted by them. We still have problems, but they don't overwhelm us.

Viewing difficulties as peace and comfort (see OTT, 115), as the Daishonin teaches us, please chant earnestly for kosen-rufu and boldly take the lead in SGI activities. Our prayers for kosen-rufu are the prayers of Buddhas and bodhisattvas.

As you willingly take on big problems and chant to find a way to solve them, you will be able to expand and elevate your state of life. And before you even notice it, all your small, trifling problems will also have been resolved in the process. This is the ultimate essence of the teaching that sufferings caused by earthly desires are a springboard to enlightenment.

Chanting Propels Us to Victory

Mr. Sato: You've often spoken of the close connection that exists between "attaining Buddhahood in this lifetime" and achieving kosen-rufu, by likening these two endeavors to the rotation of the Earth on its axis and the revolution of the Earth around the sun, respectively.

President Ikeda: In Nichiren Buddhism, chanting to resolve the problems in our own life and chanting for the realization of kosen-rufu and others' happiness are essentially one and indivisible. Both propel us forward. Our personal victories are actual proof of kosen-rufu. When we earnestly chant for the development of the SGI, which is advancing kosen-rufu, we come to develop a solid self that will not be defeated by anything. We will be able to attain the towering life state of champions.

Ms. Kumazawa: Our predecessors and seniors in the women's division have chanted with this noble vow for kosen-rufu and have—together with the first three Soka Gakkai presidents—steadfastly protected our organization.

President Ikeda: This is very true. This was particularly so at the time of the Osaka Incident,[3] when I was arrested on false charges. [President Ikeda, then Soka Gakkai youth division chief of staff, was arrested on July 3, 1957, and wrongfully charged with election law violations in a House of Councillors by-election held in Osaka. He was fully exonerated five years later.] The court case relating to the incident was weighing heavily against me, and even my attorneys told me that I should prepare myself for a guilty verdict. But the members of the women's division in Kansai were determined not to be defeated and chanted single-mindedly for my victory. And on January 25, 1962, justice indeed prevailed, with the judge acquitting me of all charges. That day is now commemorated as Kansai Women's Division Day.

Ms. Kumazawa: The members of the SGI Ikeda Kayo-kai will carry on this spirit and chant with the same resolve as the women of Ever-Victorious Kansai.

We Were All Born With a Mission

President Ikeda: Describing the Bodhisattvas of the Earth, the Lotus Sutra says that at all times "their minds are without fear" (LSOC, 260), and that they "rejoice in their hearts" (see LSOC, 255) as they freely strive in their endeavors. To live up to their teacher's aspirations for them, they exert themselves with incredible courage and vigor as if expending millions of *kalpas* of effort at every moment.

Awakening to your mission as a Bodhisattva of the Earth means coming face to face with the innermost essence of your own life. It is knowing the ultimate meaning of why you were born, why you are alive. There is no greater joy, fulfillment or pride than that which comes from awakening to your eternal mission.

While in exile on Sado Island, Nichiren declared, together with his disciples, that he felt "immeasurable delight" (WND-1, 386).

Manifesting our true identity as Bodhisattvas of the Earth represents the free and unimpeded blossoming of our self-motivation, or inner motivation. Ours is a momentous endeavor for peace that aims at fundamentally transforming the consciousness of humankind, lifting humanity to unsurpassed heights and uniting people everywhere.

Mr. Sato: Dr. David Norton (1990–95), who was a professor of philosophy at the University of Delaware in the United States, spoke of his hopes for the youth who have been fostered by you, President Ikeda, saying that the basic purpose of both religion and education is to cultivate people's self-motivation. He said he had seen proof of this in the shining eyes of the SGI youth division members, who were so enthusiastic and hopeful for the future.[4]

President Ikeda: The time has arrived when the true greatness of Nichiren Buddhism is being demonstrated around the world.

In appearance, the Bodhisattvas of the Earth are bodhisattvas struggling with the tough realities of this world. But in terms of their inner enlightenment, they are identical to Buddhas. In the same way, though the youth of the SGI may appear very ordinary, they can unfailingly bring forth from within their lives the tremendous wisdom, compassion and courage of Buddhas. You, the youth division members, are the ones who can fully demonstrate this underlying power of the Bodhisattvas of the Earth. There are no greater champions and heroes of the people. That's why you must never be defeated.

Chanting Even Once Has Incredible Power

Ms. Kumazawa: When you and Mrs. Ikeda made your first visit to the Soka Young Women's Center [in Shinanomachi, Tokyo, near the Soka Gakkai Headquarters] in June last year (2009), you chanted with us. Afterward you explained the importance of chanting with the shared commitment of mentor and disciple.

President Ikeda: In a letter to one of his young followers [Nanjo Tokimitsu], the Daishonin writes, "My wish is that all my disciples make a great vow" (WND-1, 1003). And elsewhere, he says, "The 'great vow' refers to the propagation of the Lotus Sutra" (OTT, 82). The vow to achieve kosen-rufu is the shared vow of mentor and disciple. When we unite our hearts with our mentor and chant with firm resolve, we can summon forth unimaginable power and strength.

Chanting must be followed with action. That's why it's crucial for us to chant for victory in our lives and kosen-rufu and then follow up with earnest, dedicated efforts.

Mr. Sato: Some members feel bad, because they are so busy with their jobs that they don't have time to chant as much as they'd like.

President Ikeda: There's no need to worry. You don't need to feel pressured about how much you have to chant. Even chanting Nam-myoho-renge-kyo just once has incredible power. Nichiren writes, "If you recite . . . the daimoku [even] once, then the Buddha nature of all living beings will be summoned and gather around you" (WND-1, 131). You will receive tremendous benefit from just a single, sincere utterance of Nam-myoho-renge-kyo. That's how powerful the Mystic Law is. On the other hand, just because that's true, doesn't mean we should use it as an excuse to avoid chanting! After all, as the Daishonin says, "It is the heart that is important" (WND-1, 1000).

Especially, in your youth, now is the time for you to tenaciously persevere and work harder than anyone. I hope you will show actual proof by demonstrating the power of faith in daily life and putting the teachings of Buddhism into practice in society.

Please chant vigorously and devote yourselves wholeheartedly to kosen-rufu. Confidently share your beliefs and convictions with others, and win in life. The dynamic development and victory of you, the youth of the SGI, will open the way to a bright future for all humanity.

Notes:

1. From a lecture given by Dr. Hazel Henderson in Tokyo on November 13, 2005.

2. The full passage from *The Record of the Orally Transmitted Teachings* states: "The lion's roar (*shishi ku*) is the preaching of the Buddha. The preaching of the Law means the preaching of the Lotus Sutra, or the preaching of Nam-myoho-renge-kyo in particular. The first *shi* of the word *shishi*, or 'lion' [which means 'teacher'], is the Wonderful [or Mystic] Law that is passed on by the teacher. The second *shi* [which means 'child'] is the Wonderful [or Mystic] Law as it is received by the disciples. The 'roar' [of the term *lion's roar*] is the sound of the teacher and the disciples chanting in unison" (OTT, 111).

3. Osaka Incident: The occasion when SGI President Ikeda, then Soka Gakkai youth division chief of staff, was arrested on July 3, 1957, wrongfully charged with election law violations in a House of Councillor's by-election held in Osaka earlier that year. At the end of the court case, which lasted for almost five years, he was fully exonerated.

4. From an article in the May 3, 1994, *Seikyo Shimbun.*

—————— Two ——————

Work and Faith, Part 1

Soka Gakkai Young Women's Leader Yumiko Kumazawa: Youth division members across Japan have expressed their excitement and appreciation for the first installment of this new study series, "Chanting With the Shared Vow of Mentor and Disciple." Everyone is chanting Nam-myoho-renge-kyo with a renewed sense of mission and taking action as proud Bodhisattvas of the Earth. Thank you very much, President Ikeda.

SGI President Daisaku Ikeda: I'm very happy to hear that. I've also received reports brimming with firm resolve from youth division members in the United States and other parts of the world. Young people are standing up everywhere. A fresh momentum for the victory of our kosen-rufu movement has been set in motion.

The driving force for this is Nichiren Daishonin's writings. The Daishonin states: "Without practice and study, there can be no Buddhism. You must not only persevere yourself; you must also teach others" (WND-1, 386). With that in mind, let's give our all to this study session.

Soka Gakkai Young Men's Leader Nobuhisa Tanano: Thank you very much!

We would like to take this opportunity to thank you for the tremendous encouragement you always give to the youth division behind-the-scenes support groups, including the Soka Group, Gajokai and Byakuren.

President Ikeda: They strive very hard under all manner of conditions. Where else in the world can you find young people working together with such pure dedication? Our network of Soka youth is truly refreshing. My wife and I chant Nam-myoho-renge-kyo every day for their health and safety and that each of them without exception will become happy and victorious in life.

Ms. Kumazawa: With you and Mrs. Ikeda warmly watching over us, we are doing our best each day to create a golden history of achievement. Today, we would like to ask you to talk about work, a topic of great concern to many youth division members.

President Ikeda: That is indeed a very important subject, and one with which most earnest young people will invariably grapple. Nichiren's writings provide wisdom for triumphing at work. I'll never forget how inspired I was when, as a new member, I read the passage "Regard your service to your lord as the practice of the Lotus Sutra" (WND-1, 905). The Daishonin is encouraging us to view work as part of our Buddhist practice. Work provides us with an opportunity to elevate and expand our life state. The Daishonin's words give us courage and enable us to broaden our perspective.

Mr. Tanano: Speaking of a vast life state, we are all amazed by the great achievements you have accomplished.

President Ikeda: I've worked throughout my life. Even as a boy, I worked very hard. My father suffered from debilitating rheumatism, and my four older brothers were drafted into the army, one after another. As the oldest remaining son, I would get up before dawn and help with my family's seaweed farming business. When I'd finished with that, I'd then set out on my paper route. After coming home from school, I would deliver the evening paper. The Japanese verb for "to work" *(hataraku)* originally means to bring ease (*raku*) to those around you (*hata*). I had a sense of the truth of these words from a young age.

It was also my job to deliver the seaweed my family harvested to the wholesaler. I remember proudly saying to him, "My family's seaweed is the finest there is," and him replying, "It certainly is."

Because of these experiences, I have a deep appreciation for the challenges faced by the members of the Soka Gakkai's farming communities and fishing communities divisions, as well as the pride and joy they put into their labors. Nichiren writes of "white rice grown with bone-breaking labor by the people" (WND-2, 752). The work of producing food, the very staff of life, is incredibly noble. The Daishonin understood this.

Mr. Tanano: Youth representatives of the farming communities and fishing communities divisions are sharing their experiences in faith at meetings throughout Japan. They are beacons of hope for their communities, which are facing the dual challenge of an aging population and young people moving away to work in bigger cities.

President Ikeda: I know they are making wonderful efforts. They are truly carrying out an important mission.

It's Important To Work Hard

President Ikeda: During World War II, I worked using a hammer and a lathe at Niigata Steelworks in Kamata, in Tokyo's Ota Ward. It was very grueling, physical labor.

After the war, I got a job at a printing company called Shobundo in the Nishi-Shinbashi area of Tokyo, and I attended night school while working. I remember I used to leave home at half past six in the morning. I visited customers to take their orders and was also responsible for proofreading. I gave my all to that job. The office had a warm, family-like atmosphere. I fondly remember one of my seniors telling me that it was important to take risks in life and that courage was vital. The business owner, Takeo Kurobe, was very good to me. Unfortunately, I ended up having to leave because of my poor health. Everyone expressed how sad they were to see me go.

After that, I became a clerk at the Kamata Manufacturers Association, near my home. It was a small office, but it was engaged in meaningful work, helping revive local businesses as well as medium- and small-sized factories in the area. Then I met Josei Toda, and I soon began working at his publishing company, Nihon Shogakkan. I'll never forget the sincere send-off I received from my colleagues at the Manufacturers Association when I left to work for Mr. Toda.

I'm proud to say that during my youth, whatever my job and wherever I worked, I always did my absolute best. In the writing I mentioned earlier, the Daishonin cites a commentary by the Great Teacher T'ien-t'ai on the Lotus Sutra, "No worldly affairs of life or work are ever contrary to the true reality" (WND-1, 905). This passage expresses the benefit of those who embrace the Lotus Sutra. Nothing in society or daily life is contrary to the true aspect of life. Though our efforts may seem ordinary, because they are based on faith, they shine with the light of the Mystic Law.

Nothing is nobler than striving to make the world a better place. There is no need to be overly concerned with the type of work one does, the size of the company one works for or one's position in it. Those who chant Nam-myoho-renge-kyo and endeavor each day to contribute to society are following the correct path to "attaining Buddhahood in this lifetime."

The Driving Force for Growth

Mr. Tanano: We will proudly follow your example. In the Soka Gakkai, it is often said, "In faith, do the work of one; in your job, do the work of three." How should we interpret these words and put them into practice?

President Ikeda: Basically, this refers to making effort. If you resolve to exert three times the usual effort, you'll become the driving force for growth and improvement in both your workplace and the community in which you live. Faith is what enables you to do so.

Mr. Tanano: So, as practitioners of Nichiren Buddhism, we should strive to exert ourselves that much harder.

President Ikeda: That's right. Start with prayer, and then make efforts that accord with your prayers. This is what is meant by "faith equals daily life." Every type of work requires its own kind of learning and training.

Mr. Toda was also very strict. As employees of his company, we sometimes had to go out during the day on business. It would always seem as though Mr. Toda weren't paying attention to our comings and goings, but he was. So if someone came back late, he'd bark: "You're late! Were you dawdling around somewhere?"

Once, when I returned to the office after picking up a manuscript from a writer, Mr. Toda asked me to describe the contents for him. This unexpected request made me break out in a nervous sweat. His point was that I should have used the time on the train coming back to the office to look through the manuscript and start forming an opinion on it. He was teaching me not to waste time and to work quickly and efficiently.

Ms. Kumazawa: He was always strictly training you.

President Ikeda: He was strict, but he was always right in being so. Work shapes one's character. For young people, the workplace is an important arena for doing human revolution. Those who can view things with this spirit are strong.

In his writings, Nichiren also taught his youthful follower Nanjo Tokimitsu the importance of one's attitude toward work. For example, he writes: "Being loyal to one's lord means that one never has anything to be ashamed of in serving him . . . For though one's trustworthiness may at first go unnoticed, in time it will be openly rewarded" (WND-2, 636).

Please don't engage in behavior you will regret. Please always be sincere and honest, even if no one notices your efforts. That's the key to being successful. Those who always strive to do their best at work, no matter what their position, win the greatest treasure of all—the trust of others.

Changing Poison Into Medicine

Mr. Tanano: Given the current economic crisis, people have many worries and problems where work is concerned. Some of our members are dealing with companies that are going out of business or restructuring. Others suddenly find themselves taking on heavier workloads due to staff layoffs. Still others have to work night shifts or are unable to take time off. In spite of these challenges, the youth are challenging themselves wholeheartedly with the spirit to never be defeated.

President Ikeda: I know what that's like. In my youth, I experienced the collapse of Mr. Toda's businesses. In the period of economic turmoil following World War II, many small- and medium-sized companies went bankrupt. I was in my early twenties. I know firsthand how tough it is when a company fails. Nevertheless, I stood up and ensured that the enormous debts that Mr. Toda's businesses had incurred were repaid. I struggled furiously and managed to completely transform the situation in accord with the Buddhist principle of "changing poison into medicine," thus opening the way for Mr. Toda to be inaugurated as the second president of the Soka Gakkai (in May 1951). I strove tirelessly, living the passage from *The Record of the Orally Transmitted Teachings*, "In a single moment of life we exhaust the pains and trials of millions of kalpas" (p. 214).

Mr. Tanano: Many of our members look to your youthful struggles as a source of inspiration as they face their own challenges.

President Ikeda: The present situation is extremely tough, especially for young people. With the sharp decrease in full-time job openings, things are very different from how they were just twenty or thirty years ago. In addition to individuals making efforts, we also need to evaluate and change the state of society. I can imagine the daily do-or-die struggles faced by those who run their own businesses. I'm constantly chanting for the protective forces of the universe to aid and support them.

Nichiren writes, "Iron, when heated in the flames and pounded, becomes a fine sword" (WND-1, 303). He also says, "Put into flames . . . gold becomes pure gold" (WND-1, 497). Every effort we make now will eventually become our greatest treasure. Facing and overcoming adversity causes our lives to shine like a jeweled sword or like pure gold.

Alexander Graham Bell (1847–1922), largely credited for inventing the telephone, was once asked by a journalist about the difficulty of his work. He replied: "It is pretty hard and steady work. But then, it is my pleasure, too."[1] When it comes to solving problems, there's no one ready-made magic solution. The only thing to do is to chant Nam-myoho-renge-kyo earnestly, make efforts and steadily overcome each obstacle, one after another. The same is true in the workplace. In the end, we can transform everything into something positive and good. That's what is meant by "faith for achieving absolute victory."

Ms. Kumazawa: This resonates with the well-known passage from the Daishonin's "Reply to Kyo'o": "Misfortune will change into fortune. Muster your faith, and pray to this Gohonzon. Then what is there that cannot be achieved?" (WND-1, 412).

President Ikeda: The Daishonin's words are never false. Through their courageous faith, your parents who are practicing and your seniors in faith have all shown great actual proof of victory.

Strive Heroically Amid Hard Times

Mr. Tanano: The passage you quoted earlier, "Regard your service to your lord as the practice of the Lotus Sutra" (WND-1, 905), is from Nichiren's letter "Reply to a Believer," written in 1278, at the height of the Atsuhara Persecution.

President Ikeda: That's correct. Nichiren wrote this letter when it seemed as if he might face a third exile, following the Izu Exile (in 1261) and the Sado Exile (in 1271). Discussing the prospect of being exiled a third time, he wrote, "It would bring me a hundred, thousand, ten thousand, million times greater good fortune" (WND-1, 905). Such was the towering, lionlike state of life of the Buddha of the Latter Day of the Law. And while he himself was fully prepared to undergo further persecutions, he was deeply concerned about the welfare of his disciples, who were buffeted by the adverse winds of society. His words are imbued with his impassioned spirit, as if he were saying: "Look how your teacher stands at the forefront, facing persecution head-on! As my followers, fight courageously in the place of your own mission. Triumph in your work!"

Genuine disciples of the Daishonin are never cowardly or fainthearted.

Ms. Kumazawa: Courageously showing actual proof of our Buddhist practice in society is how we can repay our debt of gratitude to our mentor.

President Ikeda: Buddhist practice takes place in the real world, in society. Nichiren writes: "The true path lies in the affairs of this world" (WND-1, 1126) and "A person of wisdom is not one who practices Buddhism apart from worldly affairs" (WND-1, 1121). We practice Nichiren Buddhism so that we can develop and improve ourselves, and carry out our human revolution in our workplaces, in our families and in our communities. We do so in order to create the greatest value where we are right now. Nichiren Buddhism is not about escaping to some other time or some imagined ideal realm. Doing so does not accord with the teaching of the Mystic Law; it is the shallow thinking of the provisional, pre-Lotus Sutra teachings. It is not reality.

Nichiren Buddhism is a living philosophy for changing reality. That is why one of the titles of the Buddha is "Hero of the World." The SGI has followed this courageous path.

The actions of the business professionals division and executives division, striving heroically amid these hard times, are also perfect examples of this.

Mr. Tanano: A youth division leader in the Kanto Region,[2] who is working at a construction company, started out as a part-time employee at age nineteen. Eventually, he was hired on as a full-time employee and, in recognition of his contributions, has received several promotions, even winning the company's President's Award. In spite of his busy professional life, whenever he has been appointed to a new leadership responsibility in the Soka Gakkai, he has challenged himself to introduce even more people to Nichiren Buddhism.

President Ikeda: That's wonderful. I'm very happy to hear stories like that. I know that hundreds of thousands, even millions, of young people are all doing their best in Japan and around the world. Nothing brings me greater joy.

Quoting a commentary by the Great Teacher Dengyo, Nichiren writes, "To discard the shallow and seek the profound is the way of a person of courage" (WND-1, 712). A true leader must be just such a "person of courage."

Notes:

1. Robert V. Bruce, *Bell: Alexander Graham Bell and the Conquest of Solitude* (Boston: Little, Brown, and Company, 1973), p. 368.

2. In the Soka Gakkai organization, the Kanto Region comprises Gumma, Ibaraki, Tochigi, Saitama and Chiba prefectures.

——————— Three ———————

Work and Faith, Part 2

Soka Gakkai Young Women's Leader Yumiko Kumazawa: Many young women have shared with me their frustration at not having enough time to participate in as many Soka Gakkai activities as they'd like because they're too busy with work.

SGI President Daisaku Ikeda: Challenging yourself to contribute to kosen-rufu, even in some small way, although you're extremely busy—that spirit is truly noble. The benefit you gain when you make an earnest effort to participate in SGI activities, even if it's only for a short time, is immense. Remember, the more challenging your circumstances, the greater the opportunity you have to grow and develop. As Nichiren Daishonin assures us, "A hundred years of practice in the Land of Perfect Bliss cannot compare to the benefit gained from one day's practice in the impure world" (WND-1, 736).

What matters is that your heart is directed toward kosen-rufu. The key is to have the attitude: "Even though I can't attend the meeting today, I'll do my utmost at work, regarding everything as part of my Buddhist practice"; or "I'm going to buckle down today so that I can finish all my work and have time on the weekend for activities"; or "No matter how busy or tired I am, I'll chant Nam-myoho-renge-kyo to support everyone's efforts, even if only a minute or two." If you have this outlook, you have already won. Such strong inner resolve will activate the protective forces of the universe and allow you to move in a positive direction without fail.

Everyone has his or her own unique situations and circumstances. I hope leaders will talk with their members, listen attentively to what they're going through in their lives, and offer concrete encouragement that will enable them to move forward with hope and courage.

Soka Gakkai Young Men's Leader Nobuhisa Tanano: I've heard that when you were the young men's division First Corps[1] leader, you were very active in the old downtown area of Tokyo. You used to cycle through the narrow backstreets of the neighborhood to visit young men who were unable to attend meetings because they were busy with work. You would also sometimes go with them to the local public bath to talk with them. And you even held informal discussions at your apartment on Sundays for those who worked long hours of overtime during the week. Through such personal encouragement, you were able to foster one person after another into a first-rate champion of kosen-rufu.

President Ikeda: Sincerity touches the hearts of others. Sometimes a few simple, encouraging words can sustain a person throughout his or her life. That is why it's so important for leaders to offer unstinting encouragement to their members.

When I would travel between Tokyo and Osaka, often by night train, I would use that time to write postcards that I would send to encourage members. In those days, we didn't have cell phones or email! If you use your minds and imaginations—which tend to be especially creative when you're young—you can find any number of ways to encourage others.

Ms. Kumazawa: In the book *Kaneko's Story*, Mrs. Ikeda talks about the challenge of balancing work and Soka Gakkai activities. She says, "I am convinced . . . that the effort to balance both organizational and other responsibilities is important for one's future, because doing so expands one's state of life, brings good fortune and vitality, and becomes the foundation for a broader, richer life experience."[2]

These words are extremely encouraging and give us all something to aspire to.

President Ikeda: The Austrian thinker Count Richard Coudenhove-Kalergi, with whom I held a dialogue, declared, "One actual step forward is worth more than a thousand imagined steps."[3] Courageously taking that first step forward in the place where you are right now is critical. Everything starts from there.

We Are Entities of the Mystic Law

Ms. Kumazawa: Some of our members are concerned because they can't enshrine the Gohonzon owing to the nature of their job or living situation—for instance, having to share a room with someone in their company dormitory and the like.

President Ikeda: A young woman who had just started practicing Nichiren Buddhism once asked second Soka Gakkai president Josei Toda about the meaning of Nam-myoho-renge-kyo. He replied with a broad smile: "That's a good question. When you get right down to it, you could say that Nam-myoho-renge-kyo is the life of Nichiren Daishonin, and your life as his disciple is also Nam-myoho-renge-kyo. Live with self-confidence, pride and optimism."

As practitioners of Nichiren Buddhism, we are entities of the Mystic Law. As such, there is no way that we will end up being unhappy. Of course, it's important for those who are unable to enshrine the Gohonzon, at present, to chant Nam-myoho-renge-kyo earnestly to be able to do so in the future, but as long as they continue practicing Nichiren Buddhism and moving forward with their fellow members, they have nothing to worry about.

Mr. Tanano: In his treatise "The Object of Devotion for Observing the Mind," the Daishonin discusses the relationship between Buddhism and worldly affairs, stating: "When the skies are clear, the ground is illuminated. Similarly, when one knows the Lotus Sutra, one understands the meaning of all worldly affairs" (WND-1, 376).

President Ikeda: Having faith in and practicing the Mystic Law enables us to freely bring forth the wisdom and creativity to succeed in life, work and various diverse endeavors in society. This is the power of Nichiren Buddhism, which is an unsurpassed teaching of life and humanity.

In today's society, where many people lack clear purpose and guiding values, you, the youth of Soka, are truly suns of hope illuminating the darkness.

Mr. Tanano: President Ikeda, you once conducted a dialogue with Karel Dobbelaere, the noted Belgian scholar of the sociology of religion. He has voiced the view that the SGI possesses one of the most essential characteristics of religion, namely, the ability to inspire people to live vibrant, joyful lives. He sees the daily practice of reciting the sutra and chanting Nam-myoho-renge-kyo as an important source of such vitality and energy. He also observed that the SGI fosters a sense of social responsibility and awareness, with members active in all spheres of society. It is promoting a movement, he said, that aims to build a global community of people who are not only interested in the development of their own societies, but also of the welfare of the world as a whole.[4]

President Ikeda: The growth of our SGI movement based on the principle that Buddhism is manifested in society is also significant from the standpoint of human history. Mr. Toda emphasized the need to foster people with a sound philosophical foundation for the sake of society, and warned us against becoming people whose faith and practice were divorced from the realities of society. He aspired for our members to develop into leaders who would contribute to their country and the world.

Genuine Buddhist practitioners are concerned not only with their own happiness, but also the happiness of others and the welfare of society, and strive to work toward those ends.

The hearts of many people these days are empty and barren inside. There are also large numbers of young people who are suffering, feeling lost and alienated, trying to find their way in the darkness.

I would like each of you, our youth division members, to be the kind of people who can impart encouragement and hope to others of your generation. May your presence shine as a spiritual safe haven or safety net for those who are struggling. It is through realizing a growing solidarity of good people in society that we will be able to change the times.

Ms. Kumazawa: Young women's division members are active in all spheres of Japanese society today, including business, education, the arts and academics. They are winning respect and appreciation for the Soka Gakkai from their employers and co-workers through their splendid examples.

President Ikeda: Our young women's division members have a great mission. Nichiren writes that women open the gateway (see WND-2, 884).

Sarah Wider, Emerson scholar and professor of English and women's studies at Colgate University in Hamilton, New York, remarked in a message to the young women's division members, who are opening the gateway to peace in their communities and in society, that just being around them makes her feel happy and that their beautiful bonds of unity are establishing the foundation for a culture of peace.[5]

When young women practicing Nichiren Buddhism stand up with firm resolve, they can completely transform their environment. That is also why it's important that, as young women, your daily speech and conduct reflect both wisdom and gracious courtesy.

Ms. Kumazawa: It's as the Daishonin says, isn't it? "The purpose of the appearance in this world of Shakyamuni Buddha, the lord of teachings, lies in his behavior as a human being" (WND-1, 852).

President Ikeda: In work, as in everything, winning in the morning is decisive. Start your day by chanting earnestly to the Gohonzon and then set off to work brimming with strong life force. Greet your colleagues with a friendly "Good morning!" As the Daishonin says, "The voice carries out the work of the Buddha" (OTT, 4). Be ready to use your voice to lift the spirits of your co-workers and brighten the atmosphere at your workplace.

You can't hope to win trust at your workplace if you frequently come in late or come in looking disheveled and unkempt. Winning in the morning is the key to winning in life.

Be Patient and Persevere

President Ikeda: Though these are troubled times, please don't allow yourselves to be defeated. Be strong and wise, and develop your abilities.

The Ikegami brothers, two of Nichiren's followers, were from a family that was engaged in construction and engineering projects for the Kamakura military government. Due to slander by their colleagues, however, they were not contracted to participate in the reconstruction of the Tsurugaoka Hachiman Shrine. In other words, they had lost a job they had been counting on.

The Daishonin wrote a letter to encourage the deeply disappointed brothers at that time, saying that this setback was surely "the design of the heavens" (WND-2, 950). In short, it definitely had some profound meaning or significance for them. He also advised: "Avoid any appearance of ill will or resentment [because of not obtaining the construction job] . . . Be sure to carry your saw and hammer in your hands or hook them at your waist, and always wear a smile" (WND-2, 950).

Don't despair when things don't go as you had hoped. Don't become depressed and feel sorry for yourself. Be patient and persevere, putting down solid roots and creating the cause for more fortunate circumstances to present themselves in the future. Faith is about putting down roots of happiness in the soil of our present reality. Eventually sprouts will appear and flowers will begin to bloom in beautiful profusion signaling the arrival of a spring of victory and success.

I know that many of our youth division members, including those of the student division, are struggling to find jobs right now. I urge them not to give up but continue doing their best.

Mr. Tanano: We, youth, are encouraging and supporting one another as we continue moving forward together.

President Ikeda: In one of his writings, the Daishonin wrote to Shijo Kingo, who was facing various obstacles, "Live so that all the people of Kamakura will say in your praise that Nakatsukasa Saburo Saemon-no-jo [Shijo Kingo] is diligent in the service of his lord, in the service of Buddhism, and in his concern for other people" (WND-1, 851).

It is the quintessential power of faith that enables one to become a great victor in life on whom others can rely and depend—be it in the sphere of work, Buddhism or society. Becoming such a victor is also brilliant proof of one's human revolution.

Notes:

1. First Corps: In the early days of the development of the Soka Gakkai in Japan, the young men's and young women's division members were organized into groups called corps, i.e. First Corps, Second Corps, etc. Daisaku Ikeda was appointed the leader of the young men's division First Corps in 1953.

2. Kaneko Ikeda, *Kaneko's Story: A Conversation with Kaneko Ikeda* (Santa Monica, California: World Tribune Press, 2008), p. 36.

3. Translated from German. R. N. Coudenhove-Kalergi, *Praktischer Idealismus* (Practical Idealism) (Vienna: Paneuropa-Verlag, 1925), pp. 164–65.

4. From an article in the January 13, 1996, *Seikyo Shimbun.*

5. From an article in the July 17, 2006, *Seikyo Shimbun.*

Four

Courage, Part 1

Soka Gakkai Youth Leader Yoshinori Sato: This March, youth division members have been energetically sharing Nichiren Daishonin's teachings with others and expanding our network of friendship. Thanks to everyone's efforts, many new people have joined our movement. Aiming toward May 3, the fiftieth anniversary of your inauguration as the third president of the Soka Gakkai, President Ikeda, the youth are giving their all to further solidifying our alliance dedicated to the cause of good.

SGI President Daisaku Ikeda: Thank you so much! Your energy and enthusiasm have ushered in a bright new age, like the morning sun rising over the horizon. I am sure this would make the Daishonin very happy. As he writes, "Anyone who teaches others even a single phrase of the Lotus Sutra is the envoy of the Thus Come One" (WND-1, 33). No youth is nobler than one dedicated to engaging tirelessly in dialogue for kosen-rufu, and realizing a peaceful and prosperous society for all.

Soka Gakkai Young Women's Leader Yumiko Kumazawa: We are confident that as long as we chant Nam-myoho-renge-kyo, take action and talk to others based on your guidance, President Ikeda, the path ahead will definitely open.

There is a young women's chapter leader from Hiroshima Prefecture who has shown a wonderful example of this. She is a person who always makes a point of greeting people brightly. One day, while waiting for the ferry to take her to work, one of her fellow passengers asked why she was always so cheerful. Summoning up her courage, she replied, "I'm cheerful because I'm a member of the Soka Gakkai." The other person then said that she wanted to be happy, too, and asked to learn more about the Soka Gakkai. Her positive reaction took the young women's division member by surprise. This encounter became the start of further dialogue, and last month, this new friend joined the Soka Gakkai.

President Ikeda: What a wonderful story! The bright confidence of our young women's division members makes them a sunlike presence in their communities and in society at large. In these times characterized by alienation and indifference, they impart hope and courage to all.

Mr. Sato: Many new members are saying that since they began practicing Nichiren Buddhism, they have become much more hopeful and positive in their everyday lives.

President Ikeda: I'm very happy to hear that. This is one of the benefits experienced by people when they first start practicing. The benefit gained by all those who warmly care for and support new members is also tremendous.

Faith in Nichiren Buddhism means being courageous. Courage is also the driving force that enables you to live the precious days of your youth victoriously and free from regret. Nichiren Buddhism is a teaching that will enable you to summon forth boundless courage.

Ms. Kumazawa: Yes, that's why we'd like to make "courage" the topic for today's discussion. In particular, we would like to ask you to talk more about the phrase *the heart of a lion king* that appears in the Daishonin's writings, as well as what it means to have "a spirit like the sun," which are words from the Ikeda Kayo-kai song, "The Vow of the Kayo-kai."

President Ikeda: The German author Johann Wolfgang von Goethe wrote, "If courage is gone—then all is gone."[1] Both on an individual level and on an organizational level, we can't win over the harsh realities of life without courage. In fact, without courage, we'll be swept away by the dark currents of the age.

As for "the heart of a lion king" and "a spirit like the sun"—these represent the Soka Gakkai spirit. It is with this spirit that we have courageously engaged in society and have won in all our endeavors.

The Daishonin declares, "Nichiren's disciples cannot accomplish anything if they are cowardly" (WND-1, 481). He is warning us that, no matter how great the Buddhist teaching we embrace, if we are cowardly we won't be able to achieve anything significant.

Summoning Forth Courage Starts With Taking a Single Step

Mr. Sato: A young man in his early twenties who has been trying to share Nichiren Buddhism with others has said that while he understands that courage is important, in reality, he finds it hard to actually be brave. He has asked what he can do to become more courageous.

President Ikeda: The key is chanting Nam-myoho-renge-kyo. Chant earnestly to bring forth courage for the sake of kosen-rufu and for your sincerity to be communicated to others. It is also important to do activities together with your seniors in faith and fellow members. It's hard to be courageous when you're by yourself. That's only human. Our organization exists so that we can continue moving forward while encouraging one another through difficult times and celebrating together when things go well.

Summoning forth courage starts with taking a single step in any aspect of your life. For example, it can be making an effort to cheerfully greet someone you'd rather avoid or making an effort to attend a meeting even when you don't feel like going. That also takes courage. By starting with small steps like these, you will be able to make great strides in your human revolution.

Ms. Kumazawa: You stress the fact that courage is crucial in "attaining Buddhahood in this lifetime."

President Ikeda: You can't overcome the "three obstacles and four devils" if you are fainthearted. Devilish functions will take advantage if you're full of fear, trepidation or hesitation. When we encounter a major obstacle, it is vital that we stand up and face it with "the heart of a lion king." This is how we awaken the life state of Buddhahood that inherently exists within our lives. Nichiren states this in his "Letter from Sado," which he wrote during the life-threatening ordeal of exile on Sado Island.

Mr. Sato: Yes. Allow me to read the passage to which you are referring. "When an evil ruler in consort with priests of erroneous teachings tries to destroy the correct teaching and do away with a man of wisdom, those with the heart of a lion king are sure to attain Buddhahood" (WND-1, 302).

President Ikeda: As we can see, the Daishonin was fully aware of the true nature of persecution befalling those who propagate the correct teaching. It arose from the plotting and scheming of jealous priests—or so-called arrogant false sages, the third and most formidable of the "three powerful enemies"—in collusion with corrupt political authorities to get rid of a person of truth and wisdom. He understood that attaining Buddhahood depended upon whether one could stand firm with the heart of a lion king when faced with such adversity. Courageous faith is the sharp sword that can defeat all devilish functions.

Mr. Sato: The persecutions and obstacles the Soka Gakkai has faced thus far have perfectly mirrored those described in Nichiren's writings.

President Ikeda: We of the Soka Gakkai and the SGI are the ones who have spread the Daishonin's teaching throughout the world exactly as he instructed. That is why we have experienced hardships like those described in his writings.

The passage you just read from "Letter from Sado" is followed by the words, "Like Nichiren, for example" (WND-1, 302).

No matter what difficulties we face, we must continue working for kosen-rufu and striving to realize peace for all humanity.

With the courageous spirit of lions, let us continue taking action, proclaiming the greatness of Nichiren Buddhism and winning in all our endeavors. This is the essence of Soka Gakkai activities.

The Latter Day of the Law is an "age of conflict"[2] in which the three poisons of greed, anger and foolishness increasingly take hold. That is why we need to be strong. We won't be able to realize our noble cause if we are timid. We need to be strong and courageous like lions, in order to protect good, hardworking people everywhere.

Courage Is Another Name for Compassion

Mr. Sato: There are far too many people who are quick to bully the weak and curry favor with the powerful. One of my friends from college was lamenting the other day that his boss at work is always pandering to his superiors while treating his subordinates in a terrible manner. Such cowardly fawning and bullying seems to me to be one of the root causes of social corruption and injustice.

President Ikeda: This is very true. That is why in "Letter from Sado," the Daishonin denounces the cowardly spirit that is the opposite of "the heart of the lion." He writes: "It is the nature of beasts to threaten the weak and fear the strong. Our contemporary scholars of the various schools are just like them" (WND-1, 302).

By rights, leaders should be the ones employing their learning and abilities to serve the people, but in reality many of them abuse their power and authority to intimidate and persecute the good and just. This is the vile nature of arrogance, at the heart of which lies cowardice.

Nichiren fought against such injustice. Even at the risk of his own life, he remonstrated against the leaders who ruled Japan at the time, bravely telling them to open their eyes to the truth and genuinely serve the welfare of the people.

Ms. Kumazawa: Why did he continue speaking out so courageously even when he knew he'd be persecuted?

President Ikeda: The Daishonin writes, "If I do not speak out I will be lacking in compassion" (WND-1, 239). Failing to proclaim the truth would have been uncompassionate, and would have meant leaving people trapped in a life of suffering and misfortune. That is why Nichiren boldly spoke out.

Speaking out in the face of injustice is an act of supreme good, of genuine compassion. Courage is just another name for compassion. The Soka Gakkai has directly inherited this spirit of the Daishonin.

First and second Soka Gakkai presidents Tsunesaburo Makiguchi and Josei Toda stood up to Japan's militarist government and were imprisoned as a result. Mr. Makiguchi died in prison. Mr. Toda was released after two years. Though forced to endure the summer heat and winter cold in his cell, as well as abuse by the prison guards, Mr. Toda never compromised his beliefs. Later, fueled by righteous indignation and determined to vindicate his great mentor, he waged a battle against the devilish forces that had caused his mentor to die in prison. He was a true lion king.

At the same time, with compassion as deep and vast as the ocean, Mr. Toda reached out to those who were suffering. He sincerely cared for each individual, tirelessly encouraging each person based on his powerful resolve to help others become happy.

Mr. Sato: During the Yubari Coal Miners Union Incident,[3] President Ikeda, you rushed to Hokkaido to support the members there. You told them that you couldn't sit by and do nothing when they, the people who were risking their lives in the mines, were being persecuted because of their faith and were suffering great hardships. Members who were in Yubari at the time have expressed how much your sincere concern meant to them.

Courage Comes From Striving With the Same Heart as Our Mentor

Ms. Kumazawa: Somehow, when we speak about the "lion king," I can't help but think of a masculine image.

President Ikeda: I believe that women are actually some of the most courageous members of our organization. Nichiren said to the lay nun Sennichi: "The Lotus Sutra is like the lion king, who rules over all other animals. A woman who embraces the lion king of the Lotus Sutra never fears any of the beasts of hell or of the realms of hungry spirits and animals" (WND-1, 949).

Faith in Nichiren Buddhism exists to enable sincere, hardworking women to live happy lives free from fear. Leaders need to vigorously proclaim this and strive to make it a reality.

Ms. Kumazawa: I find it deeply significant that the Daishonin wrote these words to Sennichi, a female disciple of strong seeking spirit. Striving in faith with the same commitment as our mentor in faith is the essence of what it means to have "the heart of the lion king," isn't it?

President Ikeda: Yes, that's right. In his famous writing, "On Persecutions Befalling the Sage," Nichiren declares, "Each of you should summon up the courage of a lion king and never succumb to threats from anyone" (WND-1, 997). He says we must "summon up" the heart of a lion king. We can't bring forth something that doesn't already exist. In other words, we all possess the heart of a lion king inside us. Faith based on the shared commitment of mentor and disciple is what enables us to summon up that inner strength.

When we strive with the same spirit as our mentor who has opened the way for kosen-rufu—that is, with the heart of a lion king—we, too, cannot fail to bring forth this courageous spirit in our lives. While assisting and supporting Mr. Toda, I made a deep vow as his disciple to follow this example and summon forth the heart of a lion king in order to protect him and surmount every obstacle we faced.

Confidently Win in Life

Ms. Kumazawa: In 1979, amid the plots hatched by the Nichiren Shoshu priesthood and others to disrupt the harmonious unity of believers [the Soka Gakkai], a Hokuriku Region[4] young women's leader courageously stood up at a meeting and declared that no matter what happened or what anyone said, you would always remain our mentor in faith, President Ikeda. Today, thirty-one years later, after a successful career as an elementary school teacher, she is now a professor at a graduate school of education, showing tremendous actual proof of faith.

President Ikeda: Yes, I know her well. She has been a wonderful role model for her juniors. I hope that all of you will summon up your courage just like she did and confidently win in life.

Mr. Sato: We will do our best. You have said: "A lion is fearless. A lion is never defeated. A lion never laments. A lion is swift. A lion vanquishes its foes." We will strive to take action with this spirit.

President Ikeda: The Daishonin also writes: "The lion king fears no other beast, nor do its cubs. Slanderers are like barking foxes, but Nichiren's followers are like roaring lions" (WND-1, 997). Now, among the members of the Soka Gakkai, we have such outstanding youth as all of you. Therefore, as long as the spirit of a lion king burns in your heart, the future of kosen-rufu will be bright and full of promise.

Notes:

1. Johann Wolfgang von Goethe, "The Same, Expanded," in *The Poems of Goethe,* translated by Edgar A. Bowring (London: John W. Parker and Son, 1853), p. 291.

2. Age of conflict: An age of quarrels and disputes. A reference to a description of the fifth five-hundred-year period in the Great Collection Sutra, which says that, in this age—which corresponds to the Latter Day of the Law—rival Buddhist schools will quarrel endlessly among themselves and Shakyamuni's correct teaching will be obscured and lost.

3. Yubari Coal Miners Union Incident (1957): A case of blatant religious discrimination in which miners in Yubari, Hokkaido, were threatened with losing their jobs on account of their belonging to the Soka Gakkai.

4. Hokuriku Region: Located along the coast of the Sea of Japan in the central region of Japan's main island.

─── Five ───

Courage, Part 2

Soka Gakkai Young Women's Leader Yumiko Kumazawa:
The Ikeda Kayo-kai song opens with the lines: "Today with you, Sensei, / With eternal brilliance in our hearts, / We cast away the winter's gloom, / Bringing spring a brand new start." Amid these dark economic times, we, the members of the young women's division, are determined to let this eternal, sunlike brilliance in our hearts shine forth all the more brightly and strongly.

SGI President Daisaku Ikeda: The sunny smiles of our young women lift the spirits of everyone around them—in their families, their workplaces and their communities. A sunlike spirit is defined by boundless courage, by hope. It is human warmth that revives people's frozen hearts. It is the light of compassion that illuminates the darkness.

This inner sun exists within the lives of all people. In a letter to Nichigen-nyo, the wife of Shijo Kingo, Nichiren Daishonin writes: "The sun breaks through the pitch-black dark" and "The Lotus Sutra is [like] the sun" (WND-1, 315). No matter how great our problems, the moment we chant Nam-myoho-renge-kyo, in accord with the principle of the "simultaneity of cause and effect," the sun of the Mystic Law rises in our hearts, and the power of the Buddha surges forth from within us.

Consequently, there is no way that you, my young friends, will end up unhappy. The more problems you have to chant about, and the more hardships you have to challenge, the more you can develop and grow, and the more brightly you will be able to shine your light on others.

Soka Gakkai Youth Leader Yoshinori Sato: In this age when the future seems so uncertain, young people are seeking a source of illumination that can guide them in the right direction. We will continue to share and spread the Daishonin's hope-filled philosophy, which teaches that "winter always turns to spring" (WND-1, 536).

President Ikeda: Yes, please do your best. The more you courageously speak to others, the more people you will help form a connection with Buddhism, and the more hope you will spread. Your voices will be a source of light that breaks through the darkness and brightly illuminates society.

Ms. Kumazawa: President Ikeda, you have spread the brilliant light of dialogue around the globe, and we will do our utmost to follow your example.

President Ikeda: Speaking of having a sunlike spirit brings to mind Natalia Sats, founder of the Moscow State Musical Theater for Children. When Mrs. Sats was in her thirties, her husband was executed in the brutal Stalinist purges that took place in the Soviet Union, and she herself was sent to a labor camp in Siberia as the wife of an "enemy of the people." But she never despaired. In fact, it was during that time of adversity that she decided she would someday establish a theater for children. And she kept this sense of purpose shining in her heart. Finally, after triumphing over countless hardships, Mrs. Sats realized her dream and dedicated the rest of her life to communicating to others the joy of living through the performing arts.

Ms. Kumazawa: Mrs. Sats once shared with a women's division member how much she treasured her encounter with you. She said that when you first visited the Moscow State Musical Theater for Children (in 1981), it was like the sun had come into the room.

President Ikeda: There is another passage about the sun from a letter the Daishonin wrote to Nichigen-nyo: "Even the darkness becomes bright when a lantern is lit . . . Can anything exceed the sun and moon in brightness? Can anything surpass the lotus flower in purity? The Lotus Sutra is the sun and moon and the lotus flower. Therefore it is called the Lotus Sutra of the Wonderful Law [Myoho-renge-kyo]" (WND-1, 186).

Each of you who upholds the Mystic Law and is dedicating your life to kosen-rufu is the sun and an embodiment of the pure lotus of the Mystic Law. This is a perfect description of the lives of the members of the Kayo-kai (Flower-Sun Group). You should therefore live your life with great pride and confidence, and let your true inner brilliance shine forth freely.

Irrespective of your circumstances, whether your job is far from exciting or far from the limelight, you can transform wherever you are into a Land of Eternally Tranquil Light, by bringing forth the brilliance of your inner Buddhahood. Your joyous presence will become a beacon of hope for others in your families, workplaces and communities.

Taking the Initiative—That's the Soka Gakkai Spirit

Mr. Sato: Many youth are making earnest efforts for kosen-rufu in rural areas throughout Japan. Most of these areas are grappling with the problem of an ever-diminishing population as more and more young people leave to work in the cities. Do you have any advice for our youth in these areas?

President Ikeda: The efforts of our youth division members who live in farming or fishing communities, or on remote, outlying islands, are truly admirable. They are extremely noble, and it is their fortune to be able to spend the days of their youth in such environments. I am sure that it can be challenging to live in a place where there are few other young people, but from another perspective, this actually gives each youth an extra opportunity to shine. People are more likely to pay attention to you as one of the few young people around! In fact, many such communities have great trust in and high expectations for Soka youth.

Mr. Sato: A zone young men's leader in northern Japan has been the head of the local basketball association for the past seven years. He organized a Village Cup Basketball Tournament and invited elementary school teams to participate. More and more students are taking part every year, and local residents are very appreciative of this effort to revitalize the community.

Many local residents are also attending various Soka Gakkai outreach activities, including seminars and introduction to Buddhism meetings, where member experiences are shared. This is giving them a deeper appreciation of the valuable contributions the youth of Soka are making to the development of the local community.

President Ikeda: That's most encouraging to hear. Having "the heart of a lion king" and "a spirit like the sun" both mean having the courage to stand alone. If the community in which you live lacks vitality, why not do something to change that? I hope that as young people, you will be resolved to make your local community the best in the whole country. Take the initiative; don't rely on others. That's the Soka Gakkai spirit.

Nichiren states, "I entrust you with the propagation of Buddhism in your province" (WND-1, 1117). From the perspective of Buddhism, where we are at present is the place we vowed to be in from the remote past in order to carry out our mission in this lifetime.

Kosen-rufu really comes down to our actions as individuals. It means to chant with concrete goals, to speak sincerely with others, to move forward steadily and to give our all each day. When we continue to make such dedicated efforts, we will definitely be joined by fellow Bodhisattvas of the Earth who share a commitment to the same noble cause. Our communities will also change, and the future will open up before us. That is the principle of bodhisattvas "emerging from the earth."

The Mystic Law Enables Us To Change Poison Into Medicine

Ms. Kumazawa: Some members are living with parents or other family members who either don't practice Nichiren Buddhism or don't approve of their participation in Soka Gakkai activities.

President Ikeda: Please don't worry if your family doesn't practice Nichiren Buddhism. Your efforts to persevere in faith in spite of opposition will ultimately become a great source of benefit for your entire family.

An Argentine proverb says, "The sun rises for everyone." If one person in a family decides to practice Nichiren Buddhism, it is as if the sun has risen to shine on his or her entire family. Through the beneficial power of faith in the Mystic Law, you will be able to lead your whole family in the direction of happiness and enlightenment. There's no need to be anxious or impatient. The power of the Mystic Law is absolute. In the end, everyone in your family will be embraced by that power.

Ms. Kumazawa: There are also members struggling with various family issues even though their whole family practices.

President Ikeda: Every family has its problems and challenges, even those who do practice. That is what enables them to grow and to write a wonderful history of faith together.

Some people may have family members who are suffering from illness. The Daishonin promises: "Nam-myoho-renge-kyo is like the roar of a lion. What sickness can therefore be an obstacle?" (WND-1, 412). From the perspective of Buddhism, everything in life has profound meaning. The

Mystic Law enables us to "change poison into medicine."

There are rainy days, snowy days and stormy days. But whatever the weather, above the clouds the sun continues to shine, and once the storm has passed, it shines even brighter. The lives of those who embrace the Mystic Law and are dedicated to kosen-rufu are like the sun.

Our fellow members in Africa cherish the proverb, "The sun rises every day." In other words, the key is to keep shining on, no matter what happens. The important thing is to keep moving forward unceasingly together with our fellow members and the Soka Gakkai, in the same way the sun continues to rise each day. When we do so, we can enter the solid upward trajectory of [the "four virtues" of] eternity, happiness, true self and purity.

Youth Have a Mission To Expand Our Hope-filled Network of Human Revolution

Mr. Sato: You have said that a lionhearted person is never careless or negligent. The youth will continue advancing vigilantly, in accord with Nichiren's words, "The lion king is said to advance three steps, then gather himself to spring, unleashing the same power whether he traps a tiny ant or attacks a fierce animal" (WND-1, 412).

President Ikeda: Lion kings never let down their guard. To always be victorious we need to give our all at every moment. Think what would happen if the sun decided it couldn't be bothered shining! When you follow the path of the "oneness of mentor and disciple," you will become lions, you will become shining suns, and you will put your lives on a course for victory throughout eternity. Herein lies the true noble brilliance of the path of the oneness of mentor and disciple.

Ms. Kumazawa: Brazilian Academy of Letters President Austregésilo de Athayde, with whom you, President Ikeda, engaged in a dialogue said to youth: "Seek out an excellent mentor in life" and "You must not be swayed by the difficulties confronting you now. You must not yield a single step to those who seek to obstruct your ideals."[1] Many champions of human rights around the world are entrusting the future to us, the youth of Soka, who have been trained by you, President Ikeda.

President Ikeda: You, the members of the youth division, have a very important mission. That is why I hope all of you, my young friends in Japan and around the world, will continue to support and encourage one another and expand our hope-filled network of human revolution to youth far and wide.

The Swiss thinker Carl Hilty (1833–1909) wrote, "The existence of light itself is an assault on darkness, for darkness cannot persist next to light."[2]

Youth of Soka, be lion kings of justice, suns of victory and champions of the stand-alone spirit!

Notes:

1. From an article in the August 23, 1993, *Seikyo Shimbun*.

2. Translated from German. Carl Hilty, *Für Schlaflose Nächte* (For Sleepless Nights) (Leipzig: J. C. Hinrichs'sche Buchhandlung, 1919), part 2, p. 227.

—— Six ——

"I Entrust the Next Fifty Years to You"

Soka Gakkai Young Men's Leader Nobuhisa Tanano: Congratulations, SGI President Ikeda, on the wonderful upcoming occasion of May 3! The growth and development of the Soka Gakkai in the fifty years since you were inaugurated as third president have been nothing short of miraculous. A leading thinker, noting that the time Shakyamuni spent expounding his teachings also spanned fifty years, has said that your achievements over that period of time in spreading Buddhism to 192 countries and territories stand as an incomparable contribution to humanity.

We, the members of the youth division, are also advancing filled with joy and pride.

SGI President Daisaku Ikeda: Thank you! Nothing makes me happier than seeing youth stand up. I entrust the next fifty years to you. You are all courageous Bodhisattvas of the Earth who have wondrously chosen to appear at this time in the twenty-first century to realize kosen-rufu. From the perspective of Buddhism, this is due to the vow that each of you has made. Each one of you has an important mission.

Soka Gakkai Young Women's Leader Yumiko Kumazawa: We of the young women's division are also engaged in an unprecedented effort to expand our network of friendship. The members of the newly established third class of the Ikeda Kayo-kai in Japan are all vibrant and brimming with energy.

President Ikeda: How happy it must make the members of the men's and women's divisions throughout Japan and around the world to see our bright youth working so hard for kosen-rufu. Youth, don't hesitate! Achieve great things to your heart's content! The future of our movement is in your hands.

Mr. Tanano: We'll do our best. President Ikeda, you assumed the presidency of the Soka Gakkai at the age of thirty-two in 1960—exactly seven hundred years after Nichiren Daishonin submitted his treatise "On Establishing the Correct Teaching for the Peace of the Land" to Hojo Tokiyori, the highest authority of the Kamakura military government, in 1260. That makes this July, the Soka Gakkai's month of youth, the seven hundred fiftieth anniversary of that occasion. The youth division is determined to celebrate this significant milestone with a great triumph. With that in mind, today, we'd like to discuss the spirit of "establishing the correct teaching for the peace of the land."

"Establishing the Correct Teaching for the Peace of the Land" in the Twenty-first Century

President Ikeda: The concept of "establishing the correct teaching for the peace of the land" is the very core of Nichiren Buddhism. As Nichikan (1665–1726), a great restorer of Nichiren Buddhism, commented, "The Daishonin's lifetime teachings are said to begin and end with 'On Establishing the Correct Teaching for the Peace of the Land.'" It's no exaggeration to say that if efforts for the goal embodied in that treatise were to be forgotten, Nichiren Buddhism would cease to exist.

Mr. Tanano: Recently, a student division member asked me about the significance of the Daishonin's treatise in modern terms, given that it was written in the thirteenth century.

President Ikeda: That's a tough question! But I'm glad that the student division members are thinking seriously about such things. It's a succinct question that strikes directly at the heart of the matter.

I believe that we are living in a time when this teaching is taking on ever-greater importance. It is an indispensable concept for attaining humanity's long-cherished wish for world peace.

Major natural disasters are occurring all around the world. The global economic crisis continues, and people are filled with uncertainty. More and more people are seeking a solid spiritual and philosophical mainstay. "Establishing the correct teaching" means setting forth what is right, raising the banner of truth and justice. It means making genuine respect for the sanctity of life our foundation. "Establishing the correct teaching" essentially comes down to young people like all of you, who embrace a truly humanistic philosophy and sound principles, standing up courageously and taking action in society.

Ms. Kumazawa: I see. So our daily efforts for kosen-rufu are directly linked to this idea of establishing the correct teaching for the peace of the land.

Some young women's division members from overseas have asked whether the "land" refers solely to Japan.

President Ikeda: Nichikan wrote that the land "encompasses the entire world and the future"[1]—in other words, it refers to all places and all times into the distant future. Countries or nations continue to change over the course of history, as do their governments and social systems. "Establishing the correct teaching for the peace of the land" represents a universal principle that includes and applies to all cultures and people on our planet.

Ms. Kumazawa: So it doesn't refer solely to the Kamakura military government.

President Ikeda: That's right. The "peace of the land" doesn't mean preserving any particular political or social system. Rather, it means ensuring the happiness of the people, and their peace and security wherever they live. We must establish the correct teaching for the peace of the land for the sake of the people, humanity and especially the youth. It is well known that the Chinese character the Daishonin used to write "land" in his treatise consists of the ideograph for "the people" enclosed in a square border. He defines the land as the place where the people live.

Mr. Tanano: I recall you discussing this point in your dialogue with Professor Jao Tsung-I (Rao Zongyi), one of China's most eminent scholars. You noted that "land" is typically written with the ideograph for "king" enclosed in a square frame suggesting a ruler's domain, but that the Daishonin mostly uses the character with the ideograph for "the people" enclosed in a square frame. Professor Jao Tsung-I was quite impressed by that fact.

President Ikeda: The people are what matter. They are the foundation. We need to build a society in which people can enjoy peaceful and secure lives, and to do that, we need to firmly establish the principles of respect for life and human dignity. Each life is precious beyond measure. We mustn't allow the tendency to diminish the value of life and human beings to prevail. Rather, it is vital that we strive to create a society that values the life and happiness of every individual. That's the practice of establishing the correct teaching for the peace of the land in the twenty-first century.

The Struggle Between the Buddha and Devilish Functions

Ms. Kumazawa: The Soka Gakkai was established eighty years ago in the period between the two world wars. When you were inaugurated as president fifty years ago, the Cold War was at its height. Against that backdrop, you boldly advocated the sanctity of life and initiated a groundswell of dialogue for peace.

President Ikeda: The Daishonin warns, "This world is the domain of the devil king of the sixth heaven" (WND-1, 495). Our world today is rampant with devilish functions that cause people to suffer and give rise to friction and social disorder. Establishing the correct teaching for the peace of the land is the struggle to vanquish those devilish functions, based on the Mystic Law, and build a realm of happiness and peace. In other words, it is a struggle between the Buddha and devilish forces, one that is fought in the lives—the hearts and minds—of each individual. Everything starts from there. That is why establishing the correct teaching for the peace of the land must begin with one-to-one dialogue.

Ms. Kumazawa: It's an endeavor to transform the human heart through dialogue, isn't it?

President Ikeda: Yes. "On Establishing the Correct Teaching for the Peace of the Land" is also written as a dialogue between a host and a guest. Nichiren writes in this treatise: "You must quickly reform the tenets that you hold in your heart and embrace the one true vehicle, the single good doctrine [of the Lotus Sutra]. If you do so, then the threefold world will become the Buddha land [a realm of peace and happiness], and how could a Buddha land ever decline? The regions in the ten directions will all become treasure realms, and how could a treasure realm ever suffer harm?" (WND-1, 25).

This itself expresses the formula for establishing the correct teaching for the peace of the land. If we care about the peace and prosperity of society, we must strive to establish a solid pillar of goodness and justice in people's hearts. Everything begins with the inner transformation of human beings themselves. We must also build a strong humanistic force for peace within society. Otherwise, the devilish nature of authority will dominate, and the cycle of suffering will be perpetuated.

Transforming the Destiny of Humanity by Transforming Ourselves

Mr. Tanano: "A great human revolution in just a single individual will help achieve a change in the destiny of a nation and further, will enable a change in the destiny of all humankind."[2] This theme of your novel *The Human Revolution* puts the idea of establishing the correct teaching for the peace of the land in contemporary terms. "Establishing the correct teaching" means doing our human revolution and "the peace of the land" could be rephrased as "a change in the destiny of all humankind."

President Ikeda: And you, the youth, are the proud protagonists working to realize that change. The Mystic Law has now spread to 192 countries and territories. The practical implementation of this concept lies in youth who uphold the Mystic Law expanding the network of human revolution throughout Japan and the world. I hope you will all strive energetically to make a vital contribution to society.

Mr. Tanano: The key, then, lies in young people who embrace a correct philosophy and possess solid conviction becoming active in every realm of human endeavor—including education, academia, the arts, business, politics and sports.

President Ikeda: That's right. Establishing the correct teaching for the peace of the land also means deepening people's understanding of Nichiren Buddhism, and expanding the number of people who appreciate its philosophy and principles. The way to spread respect for the sanctity of life and elevate the life state of all humanity is for us to engage in dialogue with as many people as possible and build an alliance dedicated to good.

Mr. Tanano: At the same time, it means opposing ideas that deny or restrict the potential of human beings and that promote discrimination.

President Ikeda: Establishing the correct teaching means refuting ideas that inflict harm and suffering. It's a struggle against that which threatens human dignity. My friend, the Argentine human rights activist Dr. Adolfo Pérez Esquivel, fought tirelessly against the brutal military regime that ruled his country. He was imprisoned for fourteen months and tortured with electric shocks, but he refused to be defeated. Eventually, there was an international outcry, and this great prisoner of conscience was released. In 1980, he was awarded the Nobel Peace Prize, and in 1983, civilian rule was restored to Argentina.

Dr. Pérez Esquivel stood up to the devilish nature of authority that objectifies human beings. His struggle to protect the sanctity of life and uphold liberty and justice inspired people everywhere. He and I are comrades in the struggle for peace and human rights, connected by bonds of deep trust.

Speaking Out Fearlessly on Behalf of the People

Ms. Kumazawa: Nichiren remonstrated with the nation's highest authorities several times, starting with the submission of his treatise "On Establishing the Correct Teaching for the Peace of the Land." He spoke out courageously, never fearing persecution.

President Ikeda: In explaining his actions, he writes, "I say all this solely for the sake of the nation, for the sake of the Law, for the sake of others, not for my own sake" (WND-1, 164). He remonstrated with the powers that be to help the people, who were suffering due to a spate of natural disasters, epidemics and famines, which the government seemed incapable of doing anything about.

It was also a struggle aimed at demonstrating the validity of his teaching. Seeking their own protection, those in power had ordered priests of the established Buddhist schools of the day to conduct prayers and rites on their behalf. These schools in turn pandered to and allied themselves with the authorities, rather than thinking of relieving the suffering of the people. This fundamental attitude had to be transformed if the people were to obtain genuine happiness and security. "On Establishing the Correct Teaching for the Peace of the Land" called for a revolution in the realm of Buddhism and secular leadership.

Mr. Tanano: The Daishonin's treatise is filled with a fierce wish to alleviate people's suffering.

President Ikeda: His remonstration included his prediction, based on the sutras, that Japan would face the "calamity of revolt within one's own domain" (internal strife) and the "calamity of invasion from foreign lands" (foreign invasion). This prediction was also founded on his desire to protect innocent people from the catastrophe of war.

Nothing is more brutal and cruel than war. I'll never forget the discussion I had with Madame Laureana Rosales, founder of Capitol University in the Philippines (in Tokyo, June 2004). She is a survivor of the infamous Bataan Death March, in which Japanese soldiers during World War II forced some seventy-five thousand allied prisoners of war to march from the Bataan Peninsula to camps thirty-seven miles away. More than twenty thousand died. Madame Rosales was only sixteen at the time. A dedicated educator, she says: "I never want to see people treating their fellow human beings with such brutality again. Education that teaches respect for the sanctity of life is indispensable for avoiding a repetition of this kind of atrocity."[3]

Ms. Kumazawa: This month (April 2010), her successor, President Casimiro B. Juarez Jr., visited the Soka International Women's Center in Shinanomachi, Tokyo, with his family, and presented you with the Laureana S. Rosales Education and Humanitarian Award. President Ikeda, we will continue to cultivate and expand the precious network of people who share our commitment for peace.

Fostering a Solid Force of Youth

President Ikeda: Founding Soka Gakkai president Tsunesaburo Makiguchi and his disciple, Josei Toda, rose up valiantly against the tide of militarism that began to sweep Japan from the early twentieth century. They were convinced that the time had come to remonstrate with the authorities. To speak out for the sake of establishing the correct teaching for the peace of the land at such a juncture meant putting their very lives on the line. Both Mr. Makiguchi and Mr. Toda were imprisoned, and their resulting struggle behind bars is truly the starting point of our organization's movement and the endeavor to realize peace based on the Daishonin's teaching.

Because of this bitter experience, Mr. Toda was only too familiar with the frightening aspects of authority. He therefore warned, "Youth must keep a close watch on the political powers!"

Mr. Tanano: You were also imprisoned on false charges, President Ikeda.[4] You have encountered momentous obstacles and unrelenting attacks, but triumphed over all of them.

President Ikeda: I have been able to do so because I based myself on the spirit of the "oneness of mentor and disciple," and the unshakable determination to establish the correct teaching for the peace of the land. Ultimately, the truth must prevail; otherwise, our goal of realizing peace will never be achieved. That is why I am deeply committed to fostering undefeatable youth who possess rock-solid conviction.

Ms. Kumazawa: We will forge ahead with strength and fortitude.

Incidentally, I heard about an experiment in which Japanese consumers who favored prestigious brand-name products were asked what they would base their purchasing decisions on if there were no brand names. They replied that they would see what everyone else bought and then buy the same.

President Ikeda: The tendency of Japanese people to be influenced by passing trends seems to remain as strong as ever. If everyone else turns to the right, they turn to the right; if everyone else looks to the left, they look to the left. This characteristic provides a breeding ground for authoritarianism and totalitarianism. British historian Arnold J. Toynbee (1889–1975) said to me, "In my opinion, the best safeguard against fascism is to establish social justice to the maximum possible extent."[5]

It's important to speak out for what is right and to remain true to one's beliefs. We must transform society from its foundations and firmly establish a philosophy of peace and human rights in the heart of each and every individual. Building a solid force of young people dedicated to that cause is the path to victory in the struggle to establish the correct teaching for the peace of the land.

Notes:

1. Translated from Japanese. Nichikan, *Rissho ankoku ron guki* (Commentary on "On Establishing the Correct Teaching for the Peace of the Land").

2. Daisaku Ikeda, *The Human Revolution* (Santa Monica, California: World Tribune Press, 2004), p. viii.

3. Translated from Japanese. From a speech delivered by Madame Rosales at Soka High School, June 7, 2004, which appeared in an article in the July 13, 2004, *Seikyo Shimbun*.

4. This refers to the Osaka Incident: The occasion when SGI President Ikeda, then Soka Gakkai youth division chief of staff, was arrested on July 3, 1957, wrongfully charged with election law violations in a House of Councillors' by-election held in Osaka earlier that year. At the end of the court case, which lasted for almost five years, he was fully exonerated on all charges in 1962.

5. Arnold Toynbee and Daisaku Ikeda, *Choose Life: A Dialogue,* edited by Richard L. Gage (Oxford: Oxford University Press, 1989), p. 226.

——— Seven ———

Transforming the Hearts and Minds of People

Soka Gakkai Young Men's Leader Nobuhisa Tanano: A Tokyo young men's division member in his early twenties recently told me his experience of trying to share Nichiren Buddhism with his friends. Struggling to do so, he received encouragement from a senior in faith who told him that in order to win his friends' understanding, it was important that he first become a true friend and ally to them.

This comment made him realize that rather than focusing, as he had been, on getting his friends to listen to what he had to say, he needed above all to listen to and understand their problems and concerns if he was going to succeed in forging genuine friendships with them. He then made a conscious decision to listen to others first. When he did this, he surprisingly found that his friends also began to pay attention to what he had to say and show an interest in his Soka Gakkai activities.

Eventually, he was able to invite four friends from his workplace to attend a rebroadcast of a nationwide youth division leaders meeting, and they found the experience very encouraging. One of his friends even subscribed to the *Seikyo Shimbun* (the Soka Gakkai's daily newspaper).

SGI President Daisaku Ikeda: The young man's efforts are to be commended. Trying to talk to people about Nichiren Buddhism in itself represents a noble effort to "establish the correct teaching for the peace of the land." There may be times when you feel frustrated in your attempts to have meaningful conversations with others, but don't be disheartened. Your seniors in the men's and women's divisions have become experts in dialogue through just such challenges, persevering and learning from the process. If everything always went smoothly from the beginning, you'd never grow and develop! Basically, everyone wants someone to listen to them and understand their problems or struggles. People are happy just to have a sympathetic ear. It takes a weight off their minds and makes them feel lighter.

Dr. Bernard Lown, one of the cofounders of the International Physicians for the Prevention of Nuclear War, with whom I've met and spoken, has said that medicine is the art of healing and listening, and that listening properly to what others are saying begins with having respect for them as individuals. He also said that friendship that is built through sincere dialogue opens the way to genuine communication.[1]

Soka Gakkai Young Women's Leader Yumiko Kumazawa: Recently, there has been a growing demand for so-called volunteer listeners or listening volunteers—people who donate their time to listen to others. This seems to be a sign of the increasing number of people in society who are suffering from loneliness and are thirsting for someone to talk to.

President Ikeda: Our Soka movement, which promotes dialogue that brings people closer together, has great significance for society as a whole.

As you know, Nichiren Daishonin's treatise "On Establishing the Correct Teaching for the Peace of the Land" is also presented in the format of a dialogue between a guest and a host. It begins with the guest lamenting the rampant turmoil and suffering of the day. The conversation unfolds with the host sincerely listening and responding to the guest's concerns and doubts.

Reaching Others' Buddha Nature Through Chanting Nam-myoho-renge-kyo

Mr. Tanano: Sometimes we find that even our closest friends aren't interested in hearing about the ideals of Buddhism or the Soka Gakkai.

President Ikeda: In "On Establishing the Correct Teaching for the Peace of the Land," there's a scene in which the guest becomes agitated when the host corrects his mistaken views. The guest basically says: "I've had it! I can't listen to this any longer!" and prepares to leave.

Mr. Tanano: It's a scene that one would normally expect to end with either the host apologizing or angrily telling the guest to leave.

President Ikeda: But the host just smiles and urges the guest to stay. He then shows understanding for the guest's feelings and concerns, patiently addressing them with reason and logic. The host's compassionate and self-assured words and his well-reasoned explanations eventually win over the guest, who in the end expresses his resolve to work together with the host toward realizing peace based on the correct teaching. The guest says, "It is not enough that I alone should accept and have faith in your words—we must see to it that others as well are warned of their errors" (WND-1, 26). The Daishonin's treatise exemplifies the ideal practice of dialogue.

Ms. Kumazawa: President Ikeda, you have held dialogues with world leaders and thinkers from many different religious backgrounds and belief systems, with the aim of realizing a peaceful and harmonious world. Your efforts are truly a monumental example of how to carry out dialogue in the modern age.

President Ikeda: First Soka Gakkai president Tsunesaburo Makiguchi spoke of three levels of friendship. He said: "Associating with people for the sake of money or material gain is shallow friendship. Being on friendly terms with someone and helping them out—for instance, recommending them for a job—is ordinary friendship. Pointing out someone's negative tendencies or warning them against error, out of genuine concern for their happiness, is noble friendship."[2]

Sometimes your efforts to share the Daishonin's teachings with your friends may be met with resistance. But your sincerity is sure to be communicated. The important thing is to engage in dialogue that is based on strong and deep prayers for your friends' happiness. Words imbued with such prayer are certain to reach the Buddha nature in the depths of their lives. Whether they are aware of it, their Buddha nature will be activated. Chanting Nam-myoho-renge-kyo enables our voice, when we speak to others, to do the Buddha's work.

To be a youth is to boldly and courageously speak out for one's beliefs. It is to engage others in dialogue for the supremely noble cause of establishing the correct teaching for the peace of the land. If you can state your convictions with a bright, confident spirit, you have succeeded.

A Passionate Call To Eliminate Nuclear Weapons

Mr. Tanano: This year, the members of the youth division in Japan are conducting a nationwide signature petition calling for the adoption of the Nuclear Weapons Convention and stirring up a groundswell for the elimination of nuclear weapons. The petition will be presented to the United Nations during the Nuclear Non-Proliferation Treaty Review Conference in May [2010].

President Ikeda: That makes me very happy. I continue to receive reports about all your vigorous efforts. The Soka Gakkai's peace movement and activities to support the United Nations, including working for the elimination of nuclear weapons, are modern expressions of the struggle to establish the correct teaching for the peace of the land.

Ms. Kumazawa: You have personally submitted proposals calling for the elimination of nuclear weapons on numerous occasions. You have also met with the leaders of such nuclear powers as the United States and Russia, as well as with several U.N. secretaries-general, in your endeavors to rid the world of the threat of nuclear weapons. We of the youth division will carry on your efforts, doing everything we can to further our movement for peace.

President Ikeda: In "On Establishing the Correct Teaching for the Peace of the Land," the Daishonin writes, "If we wish first of all to bring security to the nation and to pray for our present and future lives, then we must hasten to examine and consider the situation and take measures as soon as possible to remedy it" (WND-1, 24). The Daishonin's impassioned remonstration to the authorities was motivated by his deep wish for peace and happiness for the people. Specifically, he was speaking out to prevent the outbreak of war in the form of internal strife and foreign invasion.

War can destroy people's humanity at the very core. In particular, nuclear weapons, which in a single instant can rob the lives of hundreds of thousands of people or plunge them into hellish agony, can only be described as a product of the devilish nature inherent in life. A nuclear war could spell extinction for the human race.

Ms. Kumazawa: In his Declaration for the Abolition of Nuclear Weapons, second Soka Gakkai president Josei Toda called any person or nation that threatened the survival of humanity with the use of nuclear weapons "a devil incarnate, a fiend, a monster." [On September 8, 1957, Mr. Toda issued a declaration calling for a ban on the testing and use of nuclear weapons. The declaration, announced in a speech at a Soka Gakkai youth athletic event held in Yokohama, Japan, has become the starting point of the Soka Gakkai's activities for peace.]

President Ikeda: He did. He also said, "I want to expose and rip out the claws that lie hidden in the very depths of such weapons." What he had turned his attention to was the devilish function of disrespect for the sanctity of life lying in the inner recesses of the human heart. The Daishonin identified the same thing with the words, "Fundamental darkness manifests itself as the devil king of the sixth heaven" (WND-1, 1113). "Fundamental darkness" is the fundamental ignorance inherent in life, from which emerges disbelief in the dignity and value of human existence and a disregard for the lives of others. The greatest threat to peace is truly this fundamental ignorance.

The Daishonin says, "The single word 'belief' is the sharp sword with which one confronts and overcomes fundamental darkness or ignorance" (OTT, 119–20). The great philosophy of the Mystic Law, which teaches universal respect for life, is the means for overcoming this destructive tendency. Spreading this ideal and elevating it to the spirit of the times is the way to create lasting peace.

Building Unshakable Happiness for Ourselves and Others

Ms. Kumazawa: Recently, a young woman asked me whether there would ever be an end point in the struggle to establish the correct teaching for the peace of the land.

President Ikeda: This is probably a question that everyone asks at least once! Establishing the correct teaching for the peace of the land is—when all is said and done—a struggle to transform the hearts and minds of human beings. The battle between the forces of the Buddha and devilish functions is never over. In that sense, it is a struggle that is ongoing.

True Buddhist practice is taking action for the sake of people's happiness and peace—in other words, to establish the correct teaching for the peace of the land. This is the key to each of us "attaining Buddhahood in this lifetime" and transforming our karma or destiny. Such efforts open the way to building a firm and unshakable happiness for ourselves and others.

We are certain to meet with various obstacles in the process, however. The Daishonin's life was a series of struggles and hardships, but he demonstrated the unrivaled perseverance of One Who Can Endure, another name for a Buddha.

Mr. Tanano: The Daishonin encountered and valiantly triumphed over several life-threatening persecutions—the Matsubagayatsu Persecution (in 1260), the Izu Exile (in 1261) and the Tatsunokuchi Persecution and subsequent exile to the island of Sado (in 1271).

President Ikeda: The Daishonin declares: "Because I have expounded this teaching, I have been exiled and almost killed. As the saying goes, 'Good advice grates on the ear.' But still I am not discouraged" (WND-1, 748). His undaunted spirit is astonishing, and his words are a towering lion's roar.

Nikko Shonin, his faithful disciple and successor, inherited the Daishonin's spirit to realize peace based on the correct teaching. After the Daishonin's passing, he repeatedly remonstrated with the military government and the imperial court. He resubmitted the treatise "On Establishing the Correct Teaching for the Peace of the Land" along with a letter of remonstration signed, "Nikko, disciple of the sage Nichiren."

In contrast, the five senior priests sought to protect themselves from persecution by cowardly calling themselves "priests of the Tendai school" in a letter they submitted to the military government. [The five senior priests were five of the six senior priests designated by Nichiren Daishonin as his principal disciples. Except for Nikko, they betrayed Nichiren's teachings after his death.]

Mr. Tanano: After the deaths of Nikko and his successor Nichimoku, the spirit of establishing the correct teaching for the peace of the land quickly disappeared from the priesthood. Eventually, the priesthood lost its sense of mission and energy to work for the welfare of the people.

President Ikeda: The Soka Gakkai, an organization that has inherited the Daishonin's true teachings, has brought the long-dormant spirit of establishing the correct teaching for the peace of the land to life again in the present age. The path of this endeavor is never easy. There are many challenges along the way. We are bound to face great hardships and be buffeted by adversities. That is why we need to keep pressing forward with optimism, never giving up or becoming discouraged, no matter what happens. As long as we continue to uphold faith based on the shared commitment of mentor and disciple directly connected to the Daishonin, we will absolutely realize the lofty ideal of establishing the correct teaching for the peace of the land.

Leading thinkers around the globe have expressed the highest hopes for our movement, which seeks to enable each person to realize his or her full potential and gradually move the world in the direction of peace.

Ms. Kumazawa: Former U.N. Under-Secretary-General Anwarul K. Chowdhury conveyed his gratitude for your support of the United Nations. He declared that the SGI movement is an important expression of the power of the people. As a gathering of individuals working for peace and the development of human potential, he said, the SGI is dedicated to realizing the hopes of humanity.

President Ikeda: Establishing the correct teaching for the peace of the land is the realization of humanity's dream, the achievement of its most cherished wish of peace. I hope that you, my young friends, will continue to advance triumphantly toward that dream, day after day. When you earnestly dedicate yourself to efforts to establish the correct teaching for the peace of the land, you can manifest the power of the Buddha and bring forth your greatest strength as an individual.

This year (2010) marks the seven hundred fiftieth anniversary of the Daishonin's submission of "On Establishing the Correct Teaching for the Peace of the Land." This is a most significant time. I call on you to continue challenging your human revolution while expanding our great network dedicated to the victory of good throughout society and the world.

Notes:

1. Translated from Japanese. From an article in the June 28, 1998, *Seikyo Shimbun*.

2. Translated from Japanese. Tsunesaburo Makiguchi, *Makiguchi Tsunesaburo shingenshu* (Selected Quotes of Tsunesaburo Makiguchi), edited by Takehisa Tsuji (Tokyo: Daisanbunmei-sha, 1979), p. 26.

Eight

Study Based on *The Writings of Nichiren Daishonin* Ensures Our Victory, Part 1

Kansai Youth Leader Mitsuyuki Kumagai: SGI President Ikeda, congratulations on receiving an honorary professorship from one of China's leading academic institutions, Tsinghua University (on May 13, 2010). A number of representatives of the Kansai youth division—including the three of us, the young men's and young women's leaders and myself—were able to attend this historic ceremony recognizing your outstanding contributions to peace and friendship around the world. Thank you for allowing us to attend.

President Ikeda: Thank you. Tsinghua University President Gu Binglin and members of his delegation were impressed by the energy and solidarity of our Soka youth.

I dedicate this honor, and all the honors and awards I have received, to my mentor, second Soka Gakkai president Josei Toda. This is because the training I gained from him at "Toda University" has made me what I am today. From him I learned a wide range of subjects and profound insights into the human heart. He taught me the fundamental philosophy of life and the ultimate path of contributing to society. He was truly a great mentor. Everything I learned from Mr. Toda, I now wish to pass on to you, the youth.

Kansai Young Women's Leader Teruko Kawashima: Since last year, we of the Kansai young women's division have been studying your lectures on Nichiren Daishonin's writings and putting into practice what we have learned with the motto, "Kansai Ikeda Kayo-kai, win with *The Writings of Nichiren Daishonin!*" Through these vibrant efforts in the two ways of practice and study, capable young women are steadily being fostered. President Ikeda, Kansai will be absolutely victorious!

President Ikeda: Kansai is wonderful. You're all quite energetic. I personally built the organization in Kansai. It was the grand stage of my youth. Whenever I hear the name Kansai, I am filled with nostalgia, excitement and emotion. Ever-Victorious Kansai is the heart and mainstay of the Soka Gakkai. Kansai is the golden citadel of the "oneness of mentor and disciple," whose members have overcome all kinds of obstacles and persecutions together with me.

Kansai Young Men's Leader Yoshihiro Furuya: Our great organization in Kansai today was built through your selfless commitment to propagating the Daishonin's philosophy. We are firmly determined to carry on this legacy.

Young men's division lectures on Nichiren Buddhism in Kansai have been a great success with more than ten thousand people attending in more than one hundred seventy venues. We have also formed a training group for young men's chapter and headquarters leaders named "Ever-Victorious Academy of Buddhist Study," dedicated to studying your published lectures on *The Writings of Nichiren Daishonin.*

Mr. Kumagai: At various study meetings, the student division members are also studying the ideals and principles of Nichiren Buddhism and the practical relevance they have to society.

President Ikeda, the Kansai youth are determined to win victory after victory with the unsurpassed strategy of the Lotus Sutra that you have taught us!

Boundlessly Expand Your Capacity

President Ikeda: During the Osaka Campaign in 1956, the Kansai members united with me in studying *The Writings of Nichiren Daishonin* and striving for kosen-rufu based on its teachings. And they triumphed by exerting themselves just as the Daishonin taught. [In May 1956, the Kansai members, uniting around Daisaku Ikeda, introduced 11,111 households to Nichiren Buddhism. In elections held two months later, the Soka Gakkai-based candidate in Kansai won a seat in the Upper House, an accomplishment that was thought all but impossible at the time.]

Nichiren's writings are a wellspring of hope, a melody of joy, a jeweled sword of courage, a banner of justice and a beacon of peace. They are teachings for mentors and disciples in faith to achieve everlasting victory.

The Daishonin cites a passage from *The Words and Phrases of the Lotus Sutra* by the Great Teacher T'ien-t'ai, "One accepts [the Lotus Sutra] because of one's power of faith and continues because of one's power of constant thought" (WND-1, 471). To accept and uphold the correct teaching of Buddhism is the noblest commitment of all.

When we learn the sound life philosophy of Nichiren Buddhism, we have nothing to fear. When youth stand up with the resolve to establish the correct teaching for the peace of the land, they are invincible. Nothing can stop the advance of our gathering of ordinary people who have engraved the Daishonin's writings in their hearts and are striving with powerful conviction in faith.

Ms. Kawashima: I've heard from the pioneer members in Kansai how your impassioned lectures on *The Writings of Nichiren Daishonin* drew such an enthusiastic response from the audience that it literally shook the rickety old Kansai Headquarters building. You instilled deeply in all Kansai the importance of waging struggles for kosen-rufu based on Nichiren's writings.

President Ikeda: Mr. Toda often said: "We can find the essence of all matters in the Daishonin's writings. By basing ourselves on the highest value of the Mystic Law, we'll know how to proceed under any circumstance."

Each word and phrase in *The Writings of Nichiren Daishonin* pulses with the Daishonin's fervent wish to lead all people to enlightenment. His writings shine with a profound compassion and philosophy that can revive those in the depths of suffering and guide them toward happiness. They contain the key to victory in life and kosen-rufu, as well as a leadership philosophy based on the Mystic Law.

"Champion truth, and your strength will be doubled"—these are words I have cherished since my youth. To base oneself on *The Writings of Nichiren Daishonin* means to live by the most powerful, deep and noble truth. By doing so, you yourself can boundlessly expand your capacity. And you can win in the struggle for kosen-rufu, which opens the way to happiness and a bright future for humanity.

The Daishonin read the Lotus Sutra with his life. In the same way, the first and second presidents of the Soka Gakkai, Tsunesaburo Makiguchi and Josei Toda, read the Daishonin's writings with their lives. This is the proud tradition of the mentors and disciples of Soka.

Making the Impossible Possible

Mr. Furuya: Mr. Makiguchi was imprisoned during World War II, persecuted by the wartime Japanese militarist government for refusing to compromise his efforts to spread Nichiren Buddhism. He died in prison for his beliefs, holding high the banner of "establishing the correct teaching for the peace of the land" to the very end.

President Ikeda: In "The Opening of the Eyes," the Daishonin makes the towering declaration: "Let the gods forsake me. Let all persecutions assail me. Still I will give my life for the sake of the Law" (WND-1, 280). In his copy of the Daishonin's writings, Mr. Makiguchi underlined this passage in red. He strove just as the Daishonin taught and dedicated his life to kosen-rufu. With profound appreciation, Mr. Toda accompanied his mentor to prison and, during his two-year confinement, continued to fight for justice.

Mr. Kumagai: President Ikeda, you bore the full brunt of persecutions in Kansai, doing everything you could to protect Mr. Toda in the midst of the Osaka Incident. You vanquished all onslaughts of the three powerful enemies and laid the foundation for today's global development of kosen-rufu. We are deeply indebted to you.

President Ikeda: In "The Selection of the Time," the Daishonin declares that his teachings will spread throughout the world in the Latter Day, "Can there be any doubt that . . . the great pure Law of the Lotus Sutra will be spread far and wide throughout Japan and all the other countries of Jambudvipa [the entire world]?" (WND-1, 550). The Soka Gakkai has realized this prediction by spreading Nichiren Buddhism to 192 countries and territories around the world. The Soka Gakkai is the sole organization fulfilling the Buddha's intent and decree—triumphing over the "three obstacles and four devils" and advancing global kosen-rufu in the present age in complete accord with the Daishonin's teachings. That's why our benefits are also immeasurable.

Mr. Furuya: The Osaka Campaign saw the Soka Gakkai achieve what everyone had thought impossible. It was truly a struggle to demonstrate in society the greatness of *The Writings of Nichiren Daishonin* and the beneficial power of the Mystic Law.

President Ikeda: Mr. Toda once stated: "If you continue to uphold the Mystic Law and make steady efforts, you can definitely do your human revolution and realize kosen-rufu. This is clearly stated in *The Writings of Nichiren Daishonin*. All that's left is to make a determination and take action." Each of the members who participated in the Osaka Campaign proved the truth of these words.

Mothers of Kosen-rufu Are the Treasures of Humanity

President Ikeda: The Osaka Campaign was well before you were born, wasn't it? Did any of your family members take part?

Ms. Kawashima: My grandmother joined the Soka Gakkai in 1955 in Kyoto and later participated in the Osaka Campaign. My mother, who was an elementary school student, also joined with her. She can still vividly recall the excitement and energy of that period.

Before she started practicing Nichiren Buddhism, my mother suffered from a hearing impairment. As everyone in the family became actively involved in Soka Gakkai activities, however, she started regaining her hearing. My grandmother also received many great benefits in faith, such as overcoming tuberculosis.

From the time I was a little girl, my mother and grandmother have shared with me their joy to be working for kosen-rufu alongside you. They are both still energetically taking part in Soka Gakkai activities today.

President Ikeda: I'm very happy to hear that. Your mother and grand-mother are truly admirable.

Praising the wife of Shijo Kingo, Nichigen-nyo, the Daishonin writes: "I hear that you . . . are even firmer and more dedicated in your faith than I myself, which is indeed no ordinary matter. I wonder if Shakyamuni Buddha himself may have entered your [heart], and it moves me so that I can barely restrain my tears" (WND-1, 436). There are so many great women's division members, mothers of kosen-rufu, in Kansai, in Japan and throughout the entire world, whom I am sure the Daishonin would praise and commend in the same way. They are the Soka Gakkai's treasures; indeed, they are the treasures of humanity.

Mr. Furuya: My grandparents and my mother were members of Osaka Chapter. Since my childhood, they have always encouraged me to do my best to become a capable person who could assist you in your efforts for kosen-rufu, and they supported me in going to the Kansai Soka schools and Soka University.

Everywhere in Kansai, there are seniors in faith who, cherishing the connection they have forged with you, have shown wonderful actual proof of changing their karma and continue to give encouragement to us youth.

President Ikeda: My bonds with the Kansai members, with whom I've shared both joys and struggles, will endure on throughout the three existences—past, present and future.

The Daishonin writes in praise of Shijo Kingo's devotion, "In what lifetime could I possibly forget it?" (WND-1, 1069). Likewise, I will never forget the sincere dedication with which the Kansai members built and protected their ever-victorious citadel. Every day, together with my wife, I am chanting Nam-myoho-renge-kyo to those who fought alongside me in Kansai.

Enact the Splendid Drama of Your Youth

Mr. Kumagai: I've noticed that those who took part in the Osaka Campaign invariably say that though it was tough, it was really enjoyable. A younger member of the Kansai young men's division asked me about this, saying he thought that it seemed a contradiction in terms.

President Ikeda: Joy and suffering are inseparable. True joy is inner fulfillment and that fulfillment is gained through challenging hardships. To break through obstacles and win as a result of earnest prayer and unstinting effort—that's what makes our joy all the greater and why we feel a true sense of enjoyment. A youth spent only fretting over one's own small personal problems is sad and empty.

Kosen-rufu is a momentous endeavor to realize the happiness of all humanity. It is therefore not an easy undertaking. But, as the Daishonin writes: "Great joy [is what] one experiences when one understands for the first time that one's mind from the very beginning has been a Buddha. [Chanting] Nam-myoho-renge-kyo is the greatest of all joys" (OTT, 211–12). There is no greater joy and no greater fulfillment than practicing Nichiren Buddhism and striving for the happiness of both ourselves and others.

Mr. Furuya: On January 5, 1956, a district leaders meeting was held to kick off the Osaka Campaign. At the meeting, you noticed that many members appeared nervous and tense, so you asked for volunteers to come up to the front and dance as the other participants sang together. They were quite surprised at this suggestion.

President Ikeda: Yes, you're right. Everyone who volunteered was just improvising and dancing freely, but they put on quite a show! It really brightened up the atmosphere.

The Daishonin writes: "Even if you are not the Venerable Mahakashyapa, you should all perform a dance. Even if you are not Shariputra, you should leap up and dance. When Bodhisattva Superior Practices emerged from the earth, did he not emerge dancing?" (WND-1, 1119). Our custom of vigorously leading Soka Gakkai songs in Japan resonates with the spirit of this letter.

I led the Osaka Campaign with a determination to bring forth many more Bodhisattvas of the Earth in Osaka and every corner of Kansai.

When you challenge yourselves, please do so as if dancing serenely with the pride of a Bodhisattva of the Earth. I hope you will enact a splendid drama on the stage of Soka, the most magnificent stage for the youth.

In "On Attaining Buddhahood in This Lifetime," the Daishonin writes: "All your virtuous acts will implant benefits and roots of goodness in your life. With this conviction you should strive in faith" (WND-1, 4). All your efforts for kosen-rufu will ultimately return to you as good fortune and help you transform your karma. No efforts are more enjoyable or valuable.

We must also remember that people are drawn to where there is laughter, joy and inspiration. These kinds of elements of the human heart are really important.

My mentor, Mr. Toda, also said: "In any struggle, we have to stick with it until we can genuinely say in the end that we enjoyed it. If we can't say that, then we haven't made a real effort."

Employing the Strategy of the Lotus Sutra

Ms. Kawashima: I understand that your daily, morning lectures on *The Writings Nichiren Daishonin* at the old Kansai Headquarters during the Osaka Campaign started from eight in the morning, and members apparently attended not only from Osaka but also from all over the Kansai region.

President Ikeda: Some members even took the first train in the morning to attend. Everyone was really dedicated. I was also in earnest. That's why our hearts were united, and we could bring forth unlimited strength. I would pour my all into each lecture as if "exhausting the pains and trials of millions of kalpas" (see OTT, 214), constantly thinking how I could convey the great beneficial power of practicing Nichiren Buddhism to those who were still young in faith. When the lecture was over, everyone would leave the room surging with vigor.

I encouraged members based on the Daishonin's writings not just at the morning lectures but also at various other meetings and personal guidance sessions.

At the very beginning of the Osaka Campaign, I quoted the passage, "I am praying that, no matter how troubled the times may become, the Lotus Sutra and the ten demon daughters will protect all of you, praying as earnestly as though to produce fire from damp wood, or to obtain water from parched ground" (WND-1, 444).

Viewed from the general opinion of society, it may have seemed as though our undertaking was impossible. However, with faith and strong prayer, we could definitely make the impossible possible. I was determined to deeply instill this conviction in the hearts of our members. The Daishonin states, "Employ the strategy of the Lotus Sutra before any other" (WND-1, 1001). This was my consistent message to the members and something I personally demonstrated through my actions during the Osaka Campaign.

Mr. Furuya: Many pioneering Kansai members have remarked on how you tailored your guidance based on the Daishonin's writings according to the time or circumstances.

For instance, when you sensed that members weren't in rhythm with one another, you would emphasize the importance of solidarity, citing the passage, "If the spirit of many in body but one in mind prevails among the people, they will achieve all their goals, whereas if one in body but different in mind, they can achieve nothing remarkable" (WND-1, 618).

And when you thought the determination of an area's central leader was faltering, you would encourage the person by quoting the passage: "In battles soldiers regard the general as their soul. If the general were to lose heart, his soldiers would become cowards" (WND-1, 613).

President Ikeda: The Soka Gakkai's Buddhist study is study for the sake of practice. The purpose of reading the Daishonin's writings and studying the principles of Buddhism is so that we can encourage the person in front of us and bring forth the wisdom to overcome problems facing us, and so that we can manifest the life state of Buddhahood and together open the door to great victory. If we seriously study *The Writings of Nichiren Daishonin*, chant and take action to inspire others and help them win, the "wisdom of the truth that functions in accordance with changing circumstances" (OTT, 10) will well forth ceaselessly in our lives.

Mr. Kumagai: During the Osaka Campaign, you gave personal guidance to so many people that you must have met nearly every member in Osaka. Even at night, you would write letters and postcards to encourage members.

President Ikeda: I did everything I possibly could to encourage the members. I traveled all throughout Osaka with the fervent desire to report our victory to Mr. Toda and make him happy. I wholeheartedly encouraged each person based on the spirit of the oneness of mentor and disciple and the Daishonin's writings. That's why we won. That's what made Kansai into the great organization it is today.

If you, the youth, continue on this path, Ever-Victorious Kansai will forever grow and develop.

Nine

Study Based on *The Writings of Nichiren Daishonin* Ensures Our Victory, Part 2

Kansai Young Women's Leader Teruko Kawashima: SGI President Ikeda, I once had the opportunity to ask you how we can convey the spirit of the "oneness of mentor and disciple" to members who are new to the practice. At that time, you warmly responded: "There's no need to make it complicated. Just teach faith and practice one step at a time through your everyday interactions. Relate to them as a senior in faith and a good friend, naturally and without affectation . . . What's important is to have the intuitive wisdom of a humanistic philosopher to understand the other person's heart and choose the right time and circumstances to explain more about the practice."

I have taken this guidance as an important reference point in my faith.

SGI President Ikeda: Yes, I remember your question very well.

You don't have to put too much pressure on yourself or think that you need to be a certain way. In Nichiren Buddhism, attaining Buddhahood doesn't mean that we become something special or extraordinary. In fact, the life state of Buddhahood could simply be described as having a character that overflows with the warmest humanity.

The Lotus Sutra expounds that the nine worlds possess the potential for Buddhahood, while Buddhahood also retains the nine worlds. In other words, practicing this Buddhism doesn't mean we'll no longer experience problems or obstacles. But by earnestly chanting Nam-myoho-renge-kyo and exerting ourselves for the sake of the Law, for others and for society, we can manifest the noble life state of Buddhahood, just as we are, as our unadorned, ordinary selves. We can make the inherent nature of our lives from time without beginning shine as brilliantly as the morning sun. In *The Record of the Orally Transmitted Teachings*, Nichiren Daishonin states, "*Kuon* means something that was not worked for, that was not improved upon, but that exists just as it always has" (p. 141).

There's no need for pretension or conceit. We shouldn't compare ourselves with others and put ourselves down. The correct practice for self-actualization in Nichiren Buddhism is to contribute to society by joyfully and freely revealing our true self.

In any event, my wish is that every one of you, the members of the young women's division, becomes absolutely happy. Buddhist study exists for this purpose. Second Soka Gakkai president Josei Toda said, "Young women's division members, make study your foundation!" There is no loftier or nobler youth than one dedicated to the principle of the sanctity of life, and philosophy of peace and happiness found in Nichiren Buddhism.

Of course, I don't mean that the young men's division members can sit back and relax! I hope all of you, young men, will continue developing yourselves like master swordsmen honing their craft, and exert yourselves to put Buddhist study into action in your daily lives.

Kansai Youth Leader Mitsuyuki Kumagai: Yes, we'll do our best!

The younger members of the young men's division and the student division members are also eagerly studying the teachings of Nichiren Buddhism, especially the principle of "establishing the correct teaching for the peace of the land" that you have taught us. They are committed to leading society in a better direction, working hard to expand their network of friendship and understanding among the younger generation.

Building a Culture of Coexistence

President Ikeda: Mr. Toda was once asked during a radio interview, "Why are many young people attracted to the Soka Gakkai?" His answer was very clear. He said, "Because we have a profound philosophy."

Kansai Young Men's Leader Yoshihiro Furuya: Leaders and thinkers the world over express their high hopes for our movement's continued development, praising our efforts to open a new era in an age lacking philosophy.

Paraguayan educator and National University of Itapua president Hildegardo González Irala, who conferred an honorary doctorate on you five years ago (in April 2005), has said: "The SGI's philosophy is a guiding principle for humankind. Only through human revolution, which is being promoted under the outstanding leadership of President Ikeda, can we actualize a transformation toward a better world."[1]

President Ikeda: President González is a distinguished educator of great integrity and conviction, who has left a lasting impression on me. We have many SGI members in Paraguay, who are also admirably devoted to contributing to society.

The foundation of the lofty philosophy we are practicing is *The Writings of Nichiren Daishonin.* It is a treasure house of wisdom that can open a hopeful future for humanity. Many of the issues facing the contemporary world—such as war, violence, discrimination and environmental destruction—can ultimately be traced back to us human beings and our fundamental state of life. Nichiren Buddhism sheds light on this basic point and reveals the wisdom needed for creating a culture of genuine peace and coexistence.

In his treatise "On Establishing the Correct Teaching for the Peace of the Land," the Daishonin writes, "If we wish first of all to bring security to the nation and to pray for our present and future lives, then we must hasten to examine and consider the [dire] situation [in society] and take measures as soon as possible to remedy it" (WND-1, 24). As young people, you all have a very important mission to illuminate society and the entire world with the great philosophy of Nichiren Buddhism. It is also your right and responsibility to do so.

Develop Faith That Can Triumph Over Great Hardships

Mr. Furuya: Speaking of a struggle related to "establishing the correct teaching for the peace of the land," the Osaka Incident, in which you were arrested on false charges on July 3, 1957, remains an event deeply etched in the hearts of the Kansai members. The situation mirrored the description in the passage, "If persecutions . . . keep occurring again and again to someone who is not guilty of the slightest fault, then one should realize that that person is a true votary of the Lotus Sutra in the age after the Buddha's passing" (WND-1, 696). You strove fearlessly and won clear victory in court, being acquitted of all charges.

President Ikeda: Why does the Soka Gakkai base its activities on *The Writings of Nichiren Daishonin*? Because without the keen sword of Buddhist study, we cannot cut through obstacles and hardships.

During World War II, the militarist government's crackdown on the Soka Gakkai caused all the organization's top leaders, except first and second presidents Tsunesaburo Makiguchi and Josei Toda, to abandon their faith. As a result, the Soka Gakkai was left in a virtual state of collapse. These leaders lacked a solid foundation in Buddhist study. They began practicing Nichiren Buddhism because they were told that they would receive great benefits and become happy. But after they encountered persecution, they started to have doubts about the practice and eventually discarded their faith. There were even thankless disciples who spoke ill of Mr. Makiguchi, to whom they were greatly indebted.

However, the Daishonin clearly states in his writings: "If you propagate it [the Mystic Law], devils will arise without fail. If they did not, there would be no way of knowing that this is the correct teaching" (WND-1, 501); and "The greater the hardships befalling him [the votary of the Lotus Sutra], the greater the delight he feels, because of his strong faith" (WND-1, 33). The Daishonin explains that if we practice the correct teaching of Buddhism, we are sure to encounter obstacles. In fact, he says that facing opposition is proof that we are on the right path. Indeed, it is by triumphing over difficulties that we can construct a life state of Buddhahood imbued with indestructible happiness. This is something that the Daishonin teaches time and again in his writings.

After the war ended, Mr. Toda put special effort into promoting Buddhist study in the organization. The publication of *Nichiren Daishonin gosho zenshu* (The Complete Writings of Nichiren Daishonin) in 1952 was a crystallization of his profound determination in this sphere.

Mr. Kumagai: The Daishonin also called on his youthful disciple Nanjo Tokimitsu to develop his faith so that he could surmount all obstacles. He writes: "When those who are vital to your interests [that is, people who are important to you] try to prevent you from upholding your faith, or you are faced with great obstacles, you must believe that [Buddhist gods such as] the king Brahma and the others will without fail fulfill their vow [to protect the practitioners of the Lotus Sutra], and [you must] strengthen your faith more than ever . . . If people try to hinder your faith, I urge you strongly to feel joy" (WND-2, 566).

President Ikeda: Because he was a follower of the Daishonin, the young Tokimitsu was subjected to various criticisms by those around him and unfair treatment by the local authorities, such as having heavy taxes levied on him. However, he took on the full brunt of persecution and protected his fellow believers.

Still, the Daishonin was strict with Tokimitsu precisely because he was young. He wanted to instill in his youthful disciple the importance of having "the heart of a lion king," and taught that he could definitely win over all obstacles as long as he strove with that spirit.

The Daishonin's writings are writings for victory. We of the Soka Gakkai are practicing their very essence.

Mr. Furuya: In contrast, the corrupt priesthood has rejected and turned their backs on the Daishonin's teachings. They are guilty of the offense of trampling on the spirit of Nikko Shonin—the Daishonin's direct disciple and successor—who devoted his life to collecting and copying the Daishonin's writings, as well as lecturing on his works and letters. Their offense is equal to that of the five senior priests, who betrayed Nikko during his lifetime.

President Ikeda: In "The Twenty-six Admonitions of Nikko," Nikko writes, "Followers of this school should engrave the teachings of the Gosho [Nichiren's writings] in their lives" (GZ, 1618). Furthermore, in "On Refuting the Five Priests," he states that when the time comes to widely propagate Nichiren Buddhism, the Japanese texts of the Daishonin's writings should be translated and disseminated throughout the world (see GZ, 1613). In perfect agreement with Nikko's intent, the Soka Gakkai has translated the Daishonin's writings into various languages and spread his philosophy around the globe.

Today, there are many members joyously reading and putting into practice the Daishonin's teachings in every corner of the world. Nowhere apart from the SGI can we find such an inspiring movement of Buddhist study. This, too, is proof that our organization has directly inherited the spirit of Nichiren Daishonin and Nikko Shonin, and is advancing kosen-rufu in exact accord with the Buddha's intent and decree.

Studying Nichiren's Writings in Times of Intense Challenge

Mr. Kumagai: Even when the priesthood sent the Soka Gakkai their outrageous "Notice of Excommunication" in November 1991, they did not cite even a single passage from *The Writings of Nichiren Daishonin*. The priesthood's intent was solely to subjugate the Soka Gakkai with their traditional authority of the clergy. The Soka Gakkai, basing itself on the teachings of the Daishonin, has completely refuted this erroneous way of thinking.

President Ikeda: Mr. Toda once proclaimed, "One of the Soka Gakkai's sources of pride is that it has the world's foremost Buddhist philosophy."

It's important that we engrave the Daishonin's writings in our hearts, even if just a line or a passage, and put it into practice.

Mr. Toda also often said: "Nichiren Buddhism is extremely profound, so it's not something you can easily understand. It would benefit you more to first believe and practice this Buddhism, and later come to understand it, rather than waiting to practice it until you are convinced of it."

Ms. Kawashima: President Ikeda, in the diaries you wrote in your youth, you cited many passages from the Daishonin's writings. In an entry you made when you were twenty-one, you copied down a passage from *The Record of the Orally Transmitted Teachings*, "When one practices the Lotus Sutra [in the Latter Day of the Law] . . . difficulties will arise, and these are to be looked on as [peace and comfort]" (p. 115). Along with this passage, you added your determination: "Forge on courageously and boldly, because you are young. Always grow. Never forget to [grow dynamically]."[2] I was very moved when I read these words.

President Ikeda: No matter how busy I was—or perhaps, because I was very busy—I always made the effort to read Nichiren's writings out loud. The Daishonin didn't compose his writings in a quiet place separate from society. He wrote them amid great, life-threatening persecutions. That's why I also copied key passages in my diary, resolved that I could make them a part of my life, especially during those times of intense challenge.

I hope that you, too, when you feel deadlocked, will read the Daishonin's writings and summon forth courage from within. The Daishonin states, "The character *myo* [of Myoho-renge-kyo] means to open" (WND-1, 145). If you read his writings, you can tap the supreme wisdom for victory that exists inside you.

Those Striving on the Front Lines Are Most Important

Mr. Kumagai: During the Osaka Campaign, President Ikeda, you encouraged the members in each district in Osaka, sharing with them passages from the Daishonin's writings.

President Ikeda: That's because those striving in the districts and chapters on the front lines of kosen-rufu are most important. The Daishonin writes, "I entrust you with the propagation of Buddhism in your province" (WND-1, 1117). The district and chapter men's and women's leaders are entrusted with kosen-rufu in their communities, directly in line with this spirit of the Daishonin. The same applies to the district and chapter youth leaders. They all share deep karmic bonds from the past with the Daishonin and thus already possess tremendous good fortune.

Ms. Kawashima: I heard that on July 17, 1957, when you were released from the Osaka Detention Center after being arrested on false charges, there were many district women's leaders from Kansai and women's leaders from other regions waiting for you outside. They all rallied together, determined not to be defeated.

President Ikeda: In a letter praising a female disciple named Nichimyo who, with her small child, Oto, visited him during his exile on Sado Island, the Daishonin expresses his awe at her sincere devotion. He suggests that he must have been exiled specifically so that she could demonstrate this admirable faith (see WND-2, 1030). Similarly, whenever the Soka Gakkai has faced its severest challenges, the women's division members of Kansai have been the ones who single-mindedly chanted and strove for justice. Indeed, this has been true of all our women's division members, the mothers of kosen-rufu, in Japan and throughout the world.

Ms. Kawashima: We, the young women of the Ikeda Kayo-kai, are determined to carry on their spirit. We will proceed unerringly on this path of everlasting victory based on *The Writings of Nichiren Daishonin*, which our predecessors in Kansai walked under your leadership.

President Ikeda: Soon after I joined the Soka Gakkai, Mr. Toda personally taught me a passage from Nichiren's writings that remains an important reference point in faith for me to this day. The passage states, "If in a single moment of life we exhaust the pains and trials of millions of kalpas, then instant after instant there will arise in us the three Buddha bodies with which we are eternally endowed" (OTT, 214). And he said to me: "Champions of the Soka Gakkai must engrave this passage in their lives. Never forget this."

I always kept this passage close to my heart during the Osaka Campaign. From one point of view, "exhausting the pains and trials of millions of kalpas" begins with the self-reliant faith to take full responsibility for everything ourselves. Though we speak of victory, it isn't something easily achieved. It is only when we seriously chant, think and take action, that the great life force and wisdom not to be defeated well forth boundlessly from within. This is why I strove with the determination to make each day count for a week and each month count for a year.

In "How Those Initially Aspiring to the Way Can Attain Buddhahood through the Lotus Sutra," the Daishonin writes: "When with our mouths

95

we chant the Mystic Law [Nam-myoho-renge-kyo], our Buddha nature, being summoned, will invariably emerge. The Buddha nature of [the heavenly deities] Brahma and Shakra, being called, will protect us, and the Buddha nature of the Buddhas and bodhisattvas [throughout the universe], being summoned, will rejoice" (WND-1, 887).

We can definitely turn any situation or circumstance into a driving force for kosen-rufu through our powerful resolve.

I traveled throughout Osaka, praying with all my heart that as many people as possible in Kansai would become allies for our noble cause. In "Letter to the Lay Priest Domyo," the Daishonin cites the Lotus Sutra, "Although the devil and the devil's people will be there, they will all protect the Law of the Buddha" (WND-1, 750).

Mr. Kumagai: The members of Kansai strove hard, uniting their hearts with yours. Senior members from those days tell us how they would return home after sharing Nichiren Buddhism with others, picture the faces of those with whom they'd talked and chant Nam-myoho-renge-kyo to "glue" each person to Nichiren Buddhism with their prayer.

Now Is the Decisive Moment

President Ikeda: In a passage from "The Supremacy of the Law," which I read together with Kansai members back then, the Daishonin urges: "Strengthen your resolve more than ever. Ice is made of water, but it is colder than water. Blue dye comes from indigo, but when something is repeatedly dyed in it, the color is better than that of the indigo plant. The Lotus Sutra remains the same, but if you repeatedly strengthen your resolve [your faith], your color will be better than that of others, and you will receive more blessings than they do" (WND-1, 615).

"Repeatedly strengthen your resolve," the Daishonin says. Perseverance and tenacity are crucial in any struggle.

There will be times when things don't go as you hope. But don't let minor setbacks pull you down. Keep on pressing forward with persistence, patience and fortitude until you are victorious. The Kansai spirit is the ultimate indomitable spirit. Such unwavering power of faith and practice moves the Buddhas and heavenly deities throughout the universe, and brings forth the resolute protection that is a manifestation of the power of the Buddha and the Law.

The Daishonin writes: "This saha world is a land in which one gains the way through the faculty of hearing . . . Therefore living beings whose ears are touched by the daimoku [Nam-myoho-renge-kyo] are living beings who will gain merit" (WND-2, 87–88).

The key is to courageously tell others about our noble cause. The power of the voice can transform people's hearts. It can bring benefit and good fortune to others, and even dramatically transform a country.

The future of worldwide kosen-rufu depends on all of you, the current members of the youth division. Now is the decisive moment. Life is win or lose, and so is your youth. Buddhism exists so that you can win through all your struggles.

To his disciple [Yasaburo], who was about to face a crucial debate, the Daishonin writes: "You must simply make up your mind . . . This is where you will cross the Uji River. This is where you will ford the Seta.³ This will determine whether you win honor or disgrace your name" (WND-1, 829). Those on the side of truth must win. Only by winning can the truth prevail.

Our great shared struggle of mentor and disciple based on the Daishonin's writings will be a precious "memory of [our] present life in this human world" (WND-1, 64) and an enduring source of honor throughout the three existences—past, present and future.

Resolutely triumph in one challenge after another and boldly leave behind a golden record of your ever-victorious youth that will shine with eternal brilliance. Kansai, I'm counting on you!

Notes:

1. Translated from Japanese. From an article in the December 6, 2005, *Seikyo Shimbun*.

2. See Daisaku Ikeda, *A Youthful Diary: One Man's Journey from the Beginning of Faith to Worldwide Leadership for Peace* (Santa Monica, California: World Tribune Press, 2000), p. 10.

3. Uji River: The middle reaches of the Seta River, which originates at the southern edge of Lake Biwa and flows through Kyoto Prefecture, eventually emptying into Osaka Bay. In ancient times, it marked the southeastern line of defense for Kyoto, the capital, and was the site of several famous battles. Because of its strategic importance, whether one succeeded in crossing the Uji River determined a troop's victory or defeat. Seta, the area facing the site where this river emerges from the lake, was another strategic point of defense. Thus, "crossing the Uji River" and "fording the Seta" have the identical meaning: winning decisively.

Ten

Advancing With the Spirit of "Many in Body, One in Mind," Part 1

Soka Gakkai Young Men's Leader Nobuhisa Tanano: We are fast approaching the exciting month of July—the Soka Gakkai's traditional month of youth. In order to triumphantly celebrate the anniversary of the young men's division on July 11, we, the young men, are working solidly together to expand our network of friendship and understanding.

SGI President Ikeda: I'm happy to hear that the youth of Soka are all in high spirits.

The development of kosen-rufu depends on the passion and energy of youth. I hope all of you will forge ahead confidently with an even deeper awareness of your mission.

Soka Gakkai Young Women's Leader Yumiko Kumazawa: July 19 is the anniversary of the young women's division. We, the young women of the Ikeda Kayo-kai, are resolved to open the gateway to fresh victories of mentor and disciple.

President Ikeda: Surely nowhere in the world can we find a gathering of young people as bright, lively and filled with hope as our Soka youth.

Many youth division members are striving valiantly amid the ongoing economic recession. I hope they will overcome whatever present difficulties they may be facing, while encouraging and supporting one another. I am sending my wholehearted prayers to them, as well. My wish is for everyone to persevere and demonstrate actual proof of the Buddhist principles of "faith equals daily life" and "Buddhism is manifested in society," and to live a youth filled with boundless benefit.

Kanto Region Youth Leader Koichi Abe: We, the youth division members of the Kanto Region,[1] are also striving energetically. Fifty years ago (in 1960), the youth of Saitama Prefecture (part of the Kanto Region) were the first to call for your immediate appointment as third Soka Gakkai president. Carrying on this proud tradition of striving with a direct connection with you, we, the youth of Kanto, are determined to win in every struggle.

President Ikeda: Our Kanto members are very bright and lively. I hand built the organization in Saitama and the Kanto Region as a whole. An old Japanese proverb says, "Rule Kanto, and you rule all of Japan." Indeed, Kanto today serves as a noble center and bastion of kosen-rufu not only for Japan but also for the entire world.

Because your mission is important, your struggles will also be great. However, as Nichiren Daishonin writes to his young disciple Nanjo Tokimitsu: "Though we may suffer for a while, ultimately delight awaits us. It is like the case of a crown prince, the only son of the king. Consider this: How can he possibly fail to ascend the throne?" (WND-2, 882). The tenacious efforts you make right now will in time adorn your lives with the nobility of great monarchs.

When my mentor, second Soka Gakkai president Josei Toda, was facing dire setbacks in his businesses, I went all around Saitama to try to help resolve the situation. It was the toughest period of my youth. But because that time was very challenging, it now shines as one of the golden pages of my life.

Mr. Tanano: In your youthful diary (in October 1950), you wrote while traveling tirelessly around Saitama: "The [struggle] intensifies daily. No other choice but to forge ahead, cherishing the desire to win . . . Advance, [speak out], fight! I am young, I am young. If I do not strive now, then when again shall I have my days of youthful struggle?"[2] We, the youth, are determined to unite and create history sharing this same spirit.

In this session, President Ikeda, we'd like to ask you to talk about the spirit of "many in body, one in mind."

President Ikeda: This is an important concept that may seem straightforward to many of us, but is actually very profound. It is a cornerstone of our Buddhist practice and a vital requirement for victory in our endeavors for kosen-rufu. It's a basic point that we always need to return to.

"Strive Vigorously on the Front Lines of Kosen-rufu"

Mr. Abe: In your youth, President Ikeda, you gave a series of lectures on *The Writings of Nichiren Daishonin* to members in Saitama's Kawagoe City. They are events that Kanto members take great pride in and treasure. At these lectures, you taught the importance of uniting in the spirit of "many in body, one in mind." The guidance you gave the members back then is the source of Saitama's slogan of "Ironclad Unity."

A while ago, some leaders and members of the Kanto young men's and student divisions researched the history of your lectures in Kawagoe. They found out that you gave lectures on the Daishonin's writings to the members of Kawagoe District, in Shiki Chapter, from September 1951 to February 1953. You lectured on at least eleven of the Daishonin's writings, including "The Heritage of the Ultimate Law of Life," "Letter from Sado" and "On Persecutions Befalling the Sage."

President Ikeda: I have very fond memories of that time. I'll never forget the faces of the Kawagoe members who practiced and studied Nichiren Buddhism together with me. I was twenty-three years old when I first began giving lectures there. Mr. Toda had already been inaugurated as the Soka Gakkai's president (in May 1951), and I was delivering the lectures while continuing to shoulder full responsibility for rectifying his business situation.

Mr. Toda sternly instructed us lecturers: "It's not enough to just give a lecture. You need to infuse the participants with unwavering faith." And he continued, "Lecture confidently on my behalf!"

"On my behalf," he said. Mr. Toda was telling us to deliver the lectures as representatives dispatched directly by the Soka Gakkai president. With this awareness and responsibility, we gave the lectures in all earnestness. Every lecture was excellent training for us.

To strive vigorously on the front lines of kosen-rufu as a youthful representative of one's mentor—there can be no struggle more meaningful, no youth more radiant.

Mr. Abe: While researching the history of these lectures, I was especially surprised by the fact that you presented completion certificates to participants for each individual lecture they had attended. On the certificates are the participant's name and your name as the lecturer, the title of the writing that was studied and the date. In addition, the name of the Soka Gakkai president, Josei Toda, is printed with a large seal of the Soka Gakkai impressed next to it.

President Ikeda: I'm amazed that anyone still has them! Although they were very simple certificates, I presented them with a sincere wish for the participants' happiness and as an expression of my confidence in their future achievements and honor.

Ms. Kumazawa: The granddaughter of one participant, who kept the certificate as a family treasure, is a member of the Ikeda Kayo-kai. She is currently pursuing her graduate studies at a distinguished university in China. She recently reported that in her university, there is a Daisaku Ikeda Research Center, where study of your thought and philosophy is actively being carried out.

President Ikeda: My greatest joy is for the members with whom I strove together for kosen-rufu to enjoy great benefit, and for their families and descendents to be victorious and successful in life. Over time, the efforts we make in the realm of Buddhism, together with our fellow members, endow us with immeasurable good fortune that will shine with ever-increasing brilliance.

Exert Yourself in the Same Spirit as Nichiren Daishonin

Ms. Kumazawa: In "The Heritage of the Ultimate Law of Life," which you lectured on in Kawagoe, the Daishonin reveals the very essence of the spirit of many in body, one in mind. He writes: "All disciples and lay supporters of Nichiren should chant Nam-myoho-renge-kyo with the spirit of many in body but one in mind, transcending all differences among themselves to become as inseparable as fish and the water in which they swim. This spiritual bond is the basis for the universal transmission of the ultimate Law of life and death. Herein lies the true goal of Nichiren's propagation. When you are so united, even the great desire for widespread propagation [kosen-rufu] can be fulfilled" (WND-1, 217).

President Ikeda: This is an unforgettable passage that Mr. Toda lectured on many times. It contains an important message for all Nichiren's disciples. He declares that the heritage of the "ultimate Law of life and death" pulses and flows precisely in the efforts we make to chant Nam-myoho-renge-kyo and strive for kosen-rufu with the spirit of many in body, one in mind. The Daishonin says, "When you are so united, even the great desire for widespread propagation can be fulfilled." Indeed, working together in unity of purpose is the lifeblood of kosen-rufu. If we are united in this way, we will definitely realize that lofty goal.

Mr. Tanano: President Ikeda, I once saw a calligraphy in which you wrote with bold and dynamic strokes: "Unity Is Strength." Working for kosen-rufu with solidly united hearts is the ultimate expression of this strength of unity, isn't it?

President Ikeda: Yes, the unity taught by the Daishonin is strong and noble beyond compare.

Because the Daishonin's followers had this unity of purpose, they triumphed amid the Atsuhara Persecution.

For many years, the young Nikko Shonin, one of the Daishonin's principal disciples, spearheaded propagation efforts in Suruga Province (present-day central Shizuoka Prefecture), where Atsuhara was located. He directly conveyed the Daishonin's spirit to the farmer believers and instilled in them faith to strive in oneness with the Daishonin.

Moreover, Nikko forged strong, close-knit unity among the followers there, based on a spirit of equality and mutual respect, transcending differences such as rank, status and other social barriers. That's why he was able to construct an unshakable community of practitioners who refused to give in to any persecution or hardship.

The deaths of the three martyrs of Atsuhara, who laid down their lives for their beliefs, signaled the true establishment of an invincible Buddhism of the people.

Unity of purpose is something that must be forged by genuine disciples who base themselves on the Daishonin's spirit and boldly take their place on the front lines of the struggle. Nikko demonstrated this with his life.

Ms. Kumazawa: This heritage of solidly uniting together to achieve kosen-rufu is vibrantly alive nowhere but in the Soka Gakkai.

President Ikeda: That's right. The Soka Gakkai is an organization of members firmly united in purpose—an organization founded by presidents Tsunesaburo Makiguchi and Josei Toda for the sake of promoting kosen-rufu.

The Daishonin declares that "we win through perfect unity [i.e., the unity of many in body but one in mind]" (see WND-1, 618). At the same time, victory is also proof of solid unity of purpose.

I have won in every struggle for kosen-rufu by always making "advancing in unity" our foremost priority. This was true in the February Campaign[3] of Kamata Chapter; the effort to expand membership of the young men's First Corps; the propagation campaign in Bunkyo Chapter; the Osaka Campaign[4]; the Yamaguchi Campaign[5]; as well as the propagation efforts in Sapporo City in Hokkaido and in Tokyo's Katsushika Ward.

Mr. Tanano: At the recent April Nationwide Youth Division Leaders Meeting (held in conjunction with the Soka Gakkai Headquarters Leaders Meeting in April 2010), the members from Côte d'Ivoire called out "Unity!" and "Victory!" The members of SGI-Côte d'Ivoire—with the youth taking the lead and with "Unity!" and "Victory!" as their rallying cries—have accomplished a remarkable hundredfold increase in membership from two hundred to twenty thousand over the past twenty years.

President Ikeda: They are striving very hard. Each one of them is a supremely noble Buddha. After enduring a civil war, the members of SGI-Côte d'Ivoire have expanded their network dedicated to peace and the sanctity of life amid unimaginably harsh conditions.

Everywhere around the globe, SGI members are uniting harmoniously and winning wide trust by contributing to society as good citizens and members of their community.

Ms. Kumazawa: In countries around the world, members of the SGI Ikeda Kayo-kai are also expanding their solidly united network of young women.

Once while talking with a young woman from Europe, the subject of unity came up. She said that people who value their individuality often react negatively to concepts like "unity" or "organization," because they seem to diminish personal or individual expression. However, she said that unity in Nichiren Buddhism is based on the ideal of always cherishing each person, giving it a universality that has led it to be embraced in Europe and other parts of the world.

Shining in Our Own Unique Way

President Ikeda: That's a very important point. After all, our goal is unity in the spirit of "many in body, one in mind," not "one in body, one in mind." Everyone has his or her own precious individuality. We are all different in myriad ways—in our professions, age, gender, personality and so forth.

Gao Zhanxiang, chairman of the Chinese Culture Promotion Society in China, with whom I'm currently engaged in a dialogue, said to me that respecting one another's differences is the key to growth and progress. Indeed, it is because we are all different that we can learn from one another, allow one another's talents to shine and reveal even greater potential than we could by ourselves.

In *The Record of the Orally Transmitted Teachings*, the Daishonin states that the cherry, plum, peach and damson each embody the ultimate truth just as is, without undergoing any change (see p. 200). Nichiren Buddhism is a teaching that enables each person to fully exhibit one's unique characteristics.

Unity in diversity is born through each of us working together for the unsurpassed goal of kosen-rufu, while shining brightly in our respective places of mission. It is not something that happens as a result of a directive. It's a self-motivated unity and an alliance of people all striving to reveal their true brilliant potential.

What matters most of all is the happiness of each person and one's victory in life. One person changing his or her karma, one person's growth as a human being, is the basis for everything.

The Realm of Soka Is To Cherish Each Individual

Mr. Abe: The realm of Soka is one in which we cherish each individual and share one another's joys and struggles.

President Ikeda: The Daishonin writes: "When the pine flourishes, the cypress is overjoyed; when grasses whither, orchids weep. Even insentient plants and trees share as one a friend's joys and sorrows" (WND-2, 964).

To rejoice in our friends' happiness, to sincerely applaud their achievements, to be by their sides and encourage them when they are struggling, and to share both the good times and hard times and weather life's difficulties together with them—true unity is born from such warmhearted and humanistic ties.

Mr. Toda once explained unity very simply: "To say to another member: 'Are you also facing difficulties? Are you struggling to make ends meet, too? Are you also suffering? Then together, let's strengthen our faith!' This is what it means to be united in purpose."

The Daishonin taught the young Nanjo Tokimitsu this passage from the Lotus Sutra, "We and other living beings all together [will] attain the Buddha way" (WND-1, 1003). We attain Buddhahood "all together." When we make the vow to practice Nichiren Buddhism with others and to grow and achieve victory together, we naturally come to be solidly united in purpose.

Mr. Tanano: President Ikeda, you have taught us the spirit of always encouraging each person.

President Ikeda: That is because this is the heart of Buddhism. Day after day, I have striven to encourage countless individuals—their number now totaling in the hundreds of thousands or millions.

My wish is for every single member to become happy and proudly lead a life of victory. This is what I have lived my life for and why I continue to strive. The harmonious community of practitioners of the Soka Gakkai is the crystallization of such selfless efforts to encourage others.

Master the Eternal Leadership Principle of "Many in Body, One in Mind"

Ms. Kumazawa: May I share a story in connection with the spirit of cherishing each person? The present Kanto Region young women's leader once had the opportunity to ask you for advice about how best to interact with her father who was a nonmember for many years. In response, you encouraged her not to cause him worry and tell him what a great dad he is. She has shared that this guidance became an important turning point for her, making her self-reflect and change her attitude toward her father.

Since that time, she chanted with her mother and sister in united prayer for her father, and made a conscious effort to respect and appreciate him more. Eventually, her father decided to start practicing Nichiren Buddhism. I heard that, later on, he expressed how deeply moved he was to see firsthand so many members dedicated to supporting one another.

President Ikeda: That's truly wonderful.

It's the heart that matters. Our sincere care and earnest prayers for others will definitely reach them. Our voice and our words are also important. The Daishonin writes, "Words echo the thoughts of the mind and find expression through the voice" (WND-2, 843). Speaking out with a voice filled with compassion and conviction, or for the sake of truth, can transform the other person's heart.

In any event, in his famous writing "Many in Body, One in Mind," the Daishonin writes: "If the spirit of many in body but one in mind prevails among the people, they will achieve all their goals, whereas if one in body but different in mind, they can achieve nothing remarkable . . . Although Nichiren and his followers are few, because they are different in body, but united in mind [i.e., many in body, but one in mind], they will definitely accomplish their great mission of widely propagating the Lotus Sutra" (WND-1, 618).

The Daishonin states here that we cannot achieve victory if our minds are at cross purposes, no matter how large our group is or how much influence we possess. In contrast, even if our numbers are small, we will be able to accomplish all our goals if we are united in our shared aspiration to realize kosen-rufu.

Mr. Abe: Following the passage above, the Daishonin continues, "Though evils may be numerous, they cannot prevail over a single great [good]" (WND-1, 618). This "single great good" means working for the cause of the highest good, doesn't it?

President Ikeda: That's right. The Daishonin's writings assure us that our gathering of Buddhas dedicated to widely propagating the Mystic Law will definitely prevail in the end. The key to doing so is to advance, and to advance energetically.

For example, in a famous battle in Chinese history, King Wu of Chou led a mere eight hundred soldiers against King Chou of Yin's force of seven hundred thousand and won. King Chou's soldiers lacked firm resolve. Their indecisiveness caused them to be overwhelmed by the powerful energy of King Wu's troops, the tide of the battle swiftly turning against them (see WND-1, 618).

Only by continually taking positive action can we expand the circle of those who support our movement and foster true solidarity. Genuine unity of purpose is forged when everyone strives all out with a firm resolve to win. A passive attitude does not lead to unity. That's why one determined person standing up is the starting point of unity. It's especially important for leaders in that respect to chant earnestly and take initiative. The vigorous spirit of leaders creates a powerful momentum for victory. If in an endeavor everyone chants with shared purpose and warmly encourages one another, while pressing forward together with even greater unity, they will be able to break through all obstacles.

Now more than ever, I hope the youth will master this leadership principle of advancing with the spirit of many in body, one in mind.

Notes:

1. In the Soka Gakkai organization, the Kanto Region comprises Gunma, Ibaraki, Tochigi, Saitama and Chiba prefectures.

2. See Daisaku Ikeda, *A Youthful Diary: One Man's Journey from the Beginning of Faith to Worldwide Leadership for Peace* (Santa Monica, California: World Tribune Press, 2000), pp. 54–55.

3. February Campaign: In February 1952, President Ikeda, then an adviser to Tokyo's Kamata Chapter, initiated a dynamic propagation campaign. Together with the Kamata members, he broke through the previous monthly record of some 100 new households by introducing Nichiren Buddhism to 201 new households.

4. Osaka Campaign: In May 1956, the Kansai members, uniting around a young Daisaku Ikeda, who had been dispatched by second president Josei Toda to support them, introduced 11,111 households to the practice of Nichiren Buddhism. In elections held two months later, the Soka

Gakkai–backed candidate in Kansai won a seat in the Upper House, an accomplishment that was thought all but impossible at the time.

5. Yamaguchi Campaign: A propagation campaign that unfolded over a three-month period spanning October and November 1956 and January 1957. On the instructions of President Toda, a young Daisaku Ikeda traveled to the Chugoku region and launched an unprecedented effort to open the way for the development of the kosen-rufu movement in Yamaguchi Prefecture. At the end of September 1956, just before the campaign was launched, the Soka Gakkai had a membership of 459 households in Yamaguchi. By the end of January 1957, the number had increased almost tenfold to 4,073 households.

Eleven

Advancing With the Spirit of "Many in Body, One in Mind," Part 2

Kanto Region Youth Leader Koichi Abe: A pioneer member of the Many Treasures Group shared with us her experience of attending your lectures on *The Writings of Nichiren Daishonin* in Saitama's Kawagoe District. She described how enjoyable those days were when they enthusiastically went out to introduce others to Nichiren Buddhism, inspired by your encouragement.

She recalled one women's division member who, despite her difficult financial situation, bought a secondhand bicycle so that she could do more Soka Gakkai activities. But, every time she rode the bicycle, it created a lively "music" of squeaking and rattling. Nonetheless, she told herself that this made the ride less lonely and cheerfully continued on her way to share Nichiren Buddhism with others. As a result of such efforts, she was able to wonderfully improve her living circumstances.

SGI President Ikeda: That's very admirable.

Nichiren Daishonin writes: "A woman who takes this efficacious medicine [of Myoho-renge-kyo] will be surrounded and protected by these four great bodhisattvas [the leaders of the Bodhisattvas of the Earth] at all times. When she rises to her feet, so too will the bodhisattvas, and when she walks along the road, they will also do the same" (WND-1, 415). The women of Soka, dedicated individuals working tirelessly for kosen-rufu, will not fail to be protected by the Buddhas and bodhisattvas throughout the universe. The path they walk together with their fellow members is a golden road that will forever be imbued with the "four virtues" of eternity, happiness, true self and purity.

The Soka Gakkai Is in Accord With the Buddha's Intent and Decree

Soka Gakkai Young Women's Leader Yumiko Kumazawa: Perhaps it's a reflection of today's youth in Japan being more individualistic, but there are some youth who say that, while they don't mind practicing Nichiren Buddhism by themselves, they are reluctant to participate together with others in Soka Gakkai activities. I think how we explain the purpose of the organization becomes very important in this regard.

President Ikeda: Why do we practice Nichiren Buddhism? We practice in order to build an unshakable self, like a towering mountain, so that we can fearlessly surmount all hardships and struggles. This is what it means to attain Buddhahood in this lifetime. However, in the Latter Day that is rife with negative influences, it's nearly impossible to carry out our Buddhist practice successfully just by ourselves.

The Daishonin states: "When a tree has been transplanted, though fierce winds may blow, it will not topple if it has a firm stake to hold it up . . . Even a feeble person will not stumble if those supporting him are strong, but a person of considerable strength, when alone, may fall down on an uneven path" (WND-1, 598). Having good friends who support us is essential to upholding correct faith to the very end and leading lives of genuine victory. The Soka Gakkai is a realm of "good friends" of the kind described by the Daishonin.

Soka Gakkai Young Men's Leader Nobuhisa Tanano: I think youth is usually a period when we are easily swayed. We are also living in troubled times. In society today, it seems easy for youth to be negatively influenced and led astray.

The Soka Gakkai, however, is an oasis of happiness built through the selfless struggles of the first three presidents. I feel a deep sense of gratitude to be able to live a truly meaningful youth in this sphere of mission together with many supportive fellow members.

President Ikeda: The Soka Gakkai is a citadel of ordinary people where we honestly and freely encourage one another and strive together for happiness. The Soka Gakkai is not an organization that is artificially manufactured. It is an organization that accords with the Buddha's intent—one that presidents Tsunesaburo Makiguchi and Josei Toda devoted their lives to creating. It is a gathering that is carrying out the Buddha's decree, appearing in response to the Buddha's wish and shouldering the mission to realize kosen-rufu and lead all people to enlightenment.

Holding high the banner of "establishing the correct teaching for the peace of the land," we are unafraid of any obstacle. Indeed, we are a network of active and awakened people brimming with pride and joy.

A leading thinker has described the spread of our SGI movement around the world as "a miracle of modern history."

We mustn't forget that many among your mothers and fathers and the pioneer members of the Many Treasures Group are the ones who created this solidly united organization. Their noble names are sure to shine on eternally in the annals of human history.

Mr. Tanano: We, the youth, following in the footsteps of these countless seniors in faith, are determined to strive our hardest.

The great thing about the Soka Gakkai, as many of us have experienced, is that even if on occasion we may not feel like attending a meeting, by the time the meeting is over, we are refreshed and energized. No matter how busy we may be, when we do our best to participate in activities, our lives are strengthened and enriched.

President Ikeda: Because we are attending the foremost gathering of good friends, it's only natural that we feel energy welling forth from within. We are all good friends, each striving to do our human revolution.

In "On Establishing the Correct Teaching for the Peace of the Land," the Daishonin writes, "You have associated with a friend in the orchid room and have become as straight as mugwort growing among hemp"[1] (WND-1, 23). Our fellow members are "friends in the orchid room"—people of virtue who are positive influences. Our harmonious community of practitioners itself abounds with the power to awaken and enhance people's innate goodness.

Youth Are Promoting Worldwide Kosen-rufu

Mr. Abe: Two years ago in September (2008), with your warm support, the Saitama youth held a youth division general meeting at the Saitama Super Arena. The event was a great success with approximately thirty-six thousand members attending.

Also participating in this meeting were visiting youth representatives from Brazil who shared in our joy and excitement. Upon their return to their country, they played a central role in organizing their own youth culture general meeting in São Paulo, on May 3, 2009, with some twenty thousand participants in attendance.

President Ikeda: I've received a number of letters from those who attended that general meeting in São Paulo, stating that they have been able to introduce others to Nichiren Buddhism in the past year. This makes me very happy.

We have entered the stage in kosen-rufu where SGI youth around the world together promote our magnificent worldwide movement, applauding one another for their valiant efforts and solidly uniting in purpose. Your victory in Japan, too, will be a source of hope for members around the globe and set an example for generations to come. You have a great mission.

Mr. Abe: We will do our absolute best to win!

Ms. Kumazawa: Speaking of the development of global kosen-rufu, a Japanese young women's division member is currently working in the United States. She recently shared with me her impressions on participating in local discussion meetings there.

She described how the meetings were attended by a truly diverse group of people from all kinds of backgrounds. They engaged in cheerful and lively dialogue, and shared their determinations to advance alongside you as disciples. She said she was inspired to learn that the beautiful unity of Soka Gakkai members can be found anywhere in the world.

President Ikeda: When you view the Soka Gakkai from a global perspective, you can clearly see the deep significance it has. If you are only focused on Japan, this may be harder to understand.

The various Soka Gakkai activities you are carrying out quite naturally every day are actually shaping the times and positively transforming the world. This is the path of highest good that is known as kosen-rufu.

Mr. Tanano: Clark Strand, a respected American journalist and writer specializing in religious topics, has remarked: "The Bodhisattvas of the Earth emerged from the ground that is common to all humanity, regardless of one's race or ethnicity. Because this is so, we should be able to advance hand in hand to create a world of peace and harmony."[2]

He further added that SGI members are actively engaging in society and emulating your efforts, President Ikeda, to have open dialogue. He thinks that this is the key to the global development of the SGI that embraces people of diverse backgrounds.[3]

President Ikeda: The Soka realm of unity in diversity is one where various cultures and people harmoniously coexist.

It is an actualization of humanity's dream. Many thinking people find hope here for the possibility of changing the destiny of humankind.

The Key to Unity: A Profound Philosophy, Consistent Action and Unwavering Courage

Mr. Abe: Dr. B. N. Pande (1906–98), a renowned disciple of Mahatma Gandhi (1869–1945), once stated with a wish to change the history of human conflict: "Above all, we need to unite in order to bring harmony to humanity. I believe the Soka Gakkai plays an important role to this end."[4]

Why does the kind of unity in diversity we find in the Soka Gakkai have the power to foster human harmony?

President Ikeda: First, because our members have a profound philosophy. Second, because they take consistent action. Third, because they possess unwavering courage.

Unity in diversity—or "many in body, one in mind"—is founded upon the philosophy of the Lotus Sutra, which teaches the equality of all human beings and the sanctity of life.

In Nichiren Buddhism, there is no discrimination on the basis of race, ethnicity, class, gender or any other differences. The Daishonin declares, "A single individual has been used as an example, but the same thing applies equally to all living beings" (WND-2, 844). And he states, "There should be no discrimination between men and women" (see WND-1, 385).

We are able to have unity of purpose, because we unfailingly believe in the potential of all people to attain Buddhahood. Supreme harmony is created when everyone is able to shine his or her fullest through the power of the Mystic Law.

Ms. Kumazawa: It seems to me that many of today's Japanese leaders in society are confused and lack a sense of direction. I think the fundamental cause of this is the absence of a deep underlying philosophy and firm conviction.

As members of the young women's division, we will advance in our lives true to the guidelines you set forth for us, President Ikeda, namely: "Studying the world's foremost life philosophy" and "Engaging in dialogue to foster friendship and humanistic ideals."

President Ikeda: The more our young women's division members reach out to others in dialogue, the more they will help change the times and open a brighter future.

Why is the Soka Gakkai so strongly united? Because its members persevere in making efforts to have dialogue and exert themselves wholeheartedly for kosen-rufu. When it comes to organizational unity or harmony among humankind, the basic principle is the same.

It's important to consistently meet with others and have dialogue, creating heart-to-heart bonds—not based on our social position or title, but based on our shared humanity. It is through continuously taking such steadfast actions that genuine solidarity is born.

In our respective communities, too, our members have sincerely continued their efforts for dialogue, undeterred by even the most daunting walls of distrust. This is why we have been able to spread the Mystic Law around the globe.

Eiichi Shibusawa (1840–1931), a Japanese entrepreneur and philanthropist, said, "There is nothing in the world that is as deep and powerful as sincerity."[5] In our present-day society, in which human relationships are growing increasingly weak, sincere dialogue has become even more important.

No one valued dialogue more than Nichiren Daishonin. In his writings, he states that, in the course of spreading his doctrines, he has had occasion to meet with a great many more people than anyone else (see WND-2, 778). Similarly, all your efforts to engage others in dialogue constitute an important part of Buddhist practice directly connected to this spirit of the Daishonin.

I'm sure there will be times when you are faced with hostility or resistance. But, those experiences will make you much stronger. The Daishonin writes, "Because I have persevered without fear [against obstacles and persecutions], there are now people who think my teachings may be true" (see WND-1, 489). Even if the other person may not respond positively at that time, through persevering in dialogue with courage and sincerity, you will definitely be able to earn their trust. This trust will ultimately blossom into friendship and understanding.

Overcoming All Obstacles and Achieving Victory

Ms. Kumazawa: We are determined to resolutely protect and expand the solidly united realm of Soka, which is noble beyond compare.

President Ikeda: Buddhism is exacting. The Daishonin writes: "Strengthen your faith day by day and month after month. Should you slacken in your resolve even a bit, devils will take advantage" (WND-1, 997). Just as the Daishonin states, if we become complacent in our faith, devilish functions will take advantage. Devilish functions also seek to create division.

The Daishonin warns Munenaga, the younger of the Ikegami brothers: "Should [the two of] you fail to act in harmony, you will be like the snipe [sandpiper bird] and the shellfish who, because they were locked in combat with one another, [both] fell prey to the fisherman.

"Recite Nam-myoho-renge-kyo and take care how you behave! Take care how you behave!" (WND-2, 914).

Shortly before this, the elder Ikegami brother, Munenaka, had been disinherited by his father due to the schemes of Ryokan, a self-serving priest. Ryokan attempted to sow division between the two brothers, because they were faithful followers of the Daishonin. This is why the Daishonin stresses in his letter to the younger Munenaga that the decisive factor for victory is for the brothers and also their wives to stay solidly united.

The indestructible unity of those whose hearts are united in their shared vow for kosen-rufu, while each challenging their individual human revolution, can overcome all obstacles and achieve victories that are a brilliant testimony to the spirit of many in body, one in mind.

Mr. Abe: Three years ago (in 2007), when you visited the Saitama Ikeda Training Center, you said: "Although we speak of 'refuting the erroneous and revealing the true,' everything begins with 'refuting the erroneous.' We first need to challenge error and defeat it." We, the youth of Kanto, are determined to engrave this guidance in our lives and advance with courage and vigor.

President Ikeda: In my youth, I took the lead in setting the record straight and clarifying the truth about the Soka Gakkai throughout the Kanto Region. I strove with all my might to expand our movement for kosen-rufu and protect our members there.

"Build an invincible citadel of members in Kanto! Then, the future of kosen-rufu will be secured"—this was Mr. Toda's solemn injunction.

Our unity is that of many in body, one in mind. Here "mind" [which can also be translated as "heart"] refers to the wish for kosen-rufu, the spirit to respect our fellow members and the heart of a lion king—the ultimate expression of which is the spirit of the "oneness of mentor and disciple."

Mr. Tanano: We of the youth division will absolutely achieve great victories through faith based on the shared commitment of mentor and disciple, through continued efforts to speak out to refute the erroneous and reveal the true, and through unity based on the spirit of many in body, one in mind.

President Ikeda: When you're facing painful challenges, that's the time to vigorously chant Nam-myoho-renge-kyo. Nam-myoho-renge-kyo is like the roar of a lion king.

When others are suffering and facing difficult times, I hope that you will unsparingly use your voices to encourage them and praise them for their sincere efforts. Singing songs for kosen-rufu together can also be uplifting. Our voices are a source of strength and momentum.

The Daishonin writes, "One who perseveres through great persecutions and embraces the sutra from beginning to end is the Thus Come One's emissary" (WND-1, 942).

We must stay on guard against lapsing into the easygoing attitude to think that we've done enough and that everything will turn out fine. It's crucial to encourage one another and exert our utmost effort together to the very last moment. This is what uniting in the spirit of many in body, one in mind means. When we work together to triumph over obstacles to advance peace based on the life-affirming philosophy of Nichiren Buddhism, we are able to build an unshakable palace of happiness in our lives and an indestructible bastion of kosen-rufu.

The struggle to realize kosen-rufu for the eternal future has only just begun. Everything starts from this moment. No one can stop the unceasing flow of awakened youth who press on with unity of purpose.

The Daishonin writes: "You must summon up the great power of faith more than ever" (WND-1, 1000), and "You must raise your voice all the more and admonish [those who slander]" (WND-2, 597).

Nothing can match the strength of the network of our youth, who possess a youthful fighting spirit. I hope you will pave the way to a new era with your unstoppable advance. I am eagerly looking forward to seeing all of your magnificent youthful victories.

Notes:

1. "A friend in the orchid room" indicates a person of virtue. The implication is that the company of a virtuous person works as a good influence, just as one is imbued with fragrance on entering a room filled with orchids. It is said that mugwort supported by hemp plants grows upright.

2. From an article in the October 1, 2006, *Seikyo Shimbun*.

3. Translated from Japanese. Ibid.

4. Translated from Japanese. From an article in the May 28, 1992, *Seikyo Shimbun*.

5. Translated from Japanese. Eiichi Shibusawa, *Seien hyakuwa* (One Hundred Essays by Seien [pen name of Shibusawa]) (Tokyo: Dobunkan, 1912), p. 454.

Twelve

The Indomitable Spirit of Bodhisattva Never Disparaging

Soka Gakkai Youth Leader Yoshinori Sato: We, the youth, are striving vigorously for kosen-rufu, true to the title of the song you wrote for the youth division, "Kofu ni hashire" (Onward to Kosen-rufu).

June 30 [2010] will mark the fifty-third anniversary of the student division's establishment. Our Soka network of bright young students has now spread around the globe. Indeed, all the members of the young men's and young women's divisions are advancing filled with pride to be students of "Ikeda University."

SGI President Ikeda: Your development is a source of hope for the world. As youthful Bodhisattvas of the Earth, you shine with intelligence.

Nichiren Daishonin writes, "All phenomena that exist are manifestations of the Buddhist Law" (WND-2, 844). Everywhere, talented Soka youth are valiantly demonstrating actual proof of victory—whether it be in the sphere of learning or social contribution. There is nothing that makes me happier.

I have formed ties of friendship and promoted exchanges with universities around the globe to open a great path of peace so that you, the youth, can confidently take your place in the world.

Soka Gakkai Student Division Young Women's Leader Nobuko Oyama: Thank you very much. As your disciples, we, the members of the young women's student division, are determined to expand our network of intellect and justice throughout the world.

President Ikeda: Why did second Soka Gakkai president Josei Toda establish the student division? He wished to foster capable leaders who would genuinely serve the people and guide them in the direction of happiness and victory.

What is the difference between a humanistic leader and an authoritarian leader? An authoritarian leader looks down on the people and exploits the youth, whereas a truly humanistic leader respects the people, and works to support and foster the youth.

In the past, leaders who should have made the welfare of the people their priority let themselves be corrupted by power, growing high-handed and trampling on the happiness of countless individuals. The Japanese militarist leaders during World War II are prime examples of this.

The perversion of priorities among leaders has been the cause of the unfortunate course of history to this day. Mr. Toda entrusted the student division members who uphold the Mystic Law with the mission of fundamentally transforming this.

Soka Gakkai Student Division Young Men's Leader Takahisa Miyao: Even today, we can find many examples of individuals in high-status positions who say fine words, but in reality are concerned only with their personal interests, ridiculing ordinary people and trying to manipulate them.

The People Are the Foundation

Ms. Oyama: The early American statesman George Mason (1725–92), one of the leading proponents of the Bill of Rights, declared, "All power was originally lodged in, and is consequently derived from, the people."[1]

126

President Ikeda: The people are always the foundation. The Daishonin writes, "A king sees his people as his parents" (WND-2, 809). This means that it's important for leaders to regard the people as their parents, cherishing them and doing their utmost for them. The Daishonin also sternly notes that when "rulers of a nation . . . fail to heed or understand the afflictions of the populace," they will "sink down into the evil realms" (WND-2, 92).

Is a person great just because he or she has a high position in society or has graduated from a prestigious university? Most certainly not. Truly great are the ordinary people who work tirelessly every day for the happiness of others, for the prosperity of their communities and for the sake of peace. This is none other than the pioneer members of the Soka Gakkai and many of your parents who are dedicating themselves for kosen-rufu. These noble individuals have built today's global SGI movement through their wholehearted efforts.

I hope that you, the youth, will never forget the profound debt owed to them and become outstanding leaders committed to working for the people. That is the purpose of your studies, your Buddhist practice and the training you receive in your youth.

The members of the women's division are precious and admirable.

Mr. Miyao: If I may, I'd like to share an unforgettable experience that became a turning point in my faith.

Before entering Soka University of America, I was studying at the University of Montana. At that time, I struggled to keep up with my classes and found it hard to make friends. Nothing was going right. I became so discouraged that I started thinking about returning to Japan. That's when a pioneer women's division member of the SGI-USA encouraged me, saying: "You need to be strong! When you were in Japan, you were protected by your parents' faith. Now you have to stand up through your own faith and practice." Her words really hit home. From that point, I seriously challenged myself in both my Buddhist practice and my studies in school. I made a determination to enter SUA, and I also introduced Nichiren Buddhism to a friend.

President Ikeda: Women's division members are wonderful, aren't they? Their strength and greatness are the same everywhere. They have profound personal experiences in faith. That's why they have such solid conviction. They are admirable and precious individuals who have created a path for kosen-rufu where none existed before, striving alongside me and triumphing over all manner of obstacles. No matter how some may speak ill of them, they have sincerely continued their efforts—day in and day out in all kinds of weather—to engage others in dialogue.

Their actions mirror the practice of Bodhisattva Never Disparaging who appears in the Lotus Sutra. To one of his female disciples, the Daishonin writes: "You are a woman who is hated by others because of this teaching [of the Lotus Sutra]. You are just like Bodhisattva Never Disparaging" (WND-1, 1105).

In this session, why don't we have a discussion on Bodhisattva Never Disparaging? For the spirit of Bodhisattva Never Disparaging should also be the starting point of the youth division's efforts to convey the greatness of our movement.

Actively Reaching Out to Others

Mr. Sato: To reconfirm for readers of this session, Bodhisattva Never Disparaging appears in "Bodhisattva Never Disparaging," the 20th chapter of the Lotus Sutra. Based on his belief that all people possess the Buddha nature, he bowed and recited to each person he met the "twenty-four-character Lotus Sutra" [a passage comprising twenty-four Chinese characters in the Kumarajiva translation of the Lotus Sutra]. Namely, he would say: "I have profound reverence for you, I would never dare treat you with disparagement or arrogance. Why? Because you will all practice the bodhisattva way and will then be able to attain Buddhahood" (LSOC, 308).

President Ikeda: That's right. These words express the essential spirit of dialogue. Bodhisattva Never Disparaging bowed in respect to the Buddha nature inherent in all people's lives and recited the "twenty-four-character Lotus Sutra" to them. He actively reached out to others, even to those he saw in the distance, to speak with them.

Mr. Miyao: It seems like he had a lot of energy.

President Ikeda: There were arrogant people, however, who resented and ridiculed him. They couldn't believe in the Lotus Sutra's life-affirming philosophy and teaching that all people have the potential for Buddhahood. They instead attacked him, beating him with sticks or pelting him with stones. Yet, he never ceased his practice of venerating others. He refused to disparage anyone. This is why he is called Bodhisattva Never Disparaging.

Mr. Miyao: So, no matter how much he was maligned or persecuted, he never stopped carrying out his Buddhist practice, right?

President Ikeda: That's correct. This is what makes Bodhisattva Never Disparaging so admirable. He courageously sought out arrogant people who were contemptuous of others. He never gave up. He kept on striving. In short, he had great perseverance. These are not actions of one who is passive.

The Daishonin states, "[Bodhisattva Never Disparaging] was a practitioner at the initial stage of rejoicing"[2] (WND-1, 474). The "initial stage of rejoicing" is the level of practice attained by someone who, in the time after the Buddha's passing, rejoices upon hearing the Lotus Sutra.

Bodhisattva Never Disparaging felt genuine joy at having encountered the ultimate truth of the Lotus Sutra. That's why he remained steadfast in his faith. In a sense, all of you, the members of the youth and student divisions today, are carrying on this spirit of Bodhisattva Never Disparaging in your activities.

Please Keep Safe and Free of Accidents

Mr. Sato: We, the youth, are determined to strive resolutely, never forgetting our original spirit.

Bodhisattva Never Disparaging was certainly very wise. When others made an attempt to attack him with sticks and stones, he would run off to a safe distance, and then recite out loud the "twenty-four-character Lotus Sutra" so that everyone could still hear it.

President Ikeda: He had an unwavering commitment to the truth. That's why he could be so cheerful and open-minded in his actions.

We are living in what Buddhism calls an evil age defiled by the five impurities [of the age, of desire, of living beings, of thought (or view) and of life span]. The number of dishonest, corrupt people in society seems to be increasing. We mustn't be deceived by them or get entangled in their evil deeds. Youth need to possess keen wisdom not to allow negative influences to affect their lives. I hope you will all be strong and discerning individuals.

The Daishonin writes, "Be millions of times more careful than ever" (WND-1, 839). I especially hope that all our young women's division members will exercise caution and keep safe and free of accidents.

Ms. Oyama: Yes. We will always remind one another to follow your advice about staying alert and not getting home too late at night.

Buddhism Is a Philosophy for Reviving the Human Spirit

Mr. Miyao: Once, the renowned Buddhist scholar Dr. Surya B. Shakya (1925–99) of Nepal stated in his dialogue with you (in November 1992): "Bodhisattva Never Disparaging carried through with his practice of venerating others, convinced that all living beings possess the Buddha nature. To have conviction in the Buddha nature of all living beings and to take action to reveal it—here we find a supreme philosophy for perfecting one's character."[3]

Furthermore, he commented that the SGI, guided by your leadership, is an organization that practices and spreads this bodhisattva way in the modern age.[4]

President Ikeda: Dr. Shakya was a prominent intellectual of Nepal, the land of Shakyamuni's birth. I will never forget meeting and talking with him.

Ms. Oyama: President Ikeda, why did Bodhisattva Never Disparaging dauntlessly persevere in his practice, even though he faced so many persecutions?

President Ikeda: Bodhisattva Never Disparaging lived at the end of the Middle Day of the Law after the passing of Buddha Awesome Sound King.[5] That Buddha's true teachings had long been forgotten and society was filled with arrogant monks. In such confusing times, Bodhisattva Never Disparaging deeply rejoiced on hearing the essence of the Buddha's teachings and sought to revive it in the lives of others.

"I must not let the Buddha's teaching disappear!" "Just as the Buddha taught, I will lead all people to enlightenment!" I'm sure it was this kind of ardent desire that motivated Bodhisattva Never Disparaging to remain undeterred in his practice.

As Dr. Shakya said, Bodhisattva Never Disparaging's practice embodies a supreme philosophy for reviving the human spirit. Our SGI movement, based on the shared commitment of mentor and disciple, is also an endeavor to restore this great teaching of respect for others in the evil age of the Latter Day.

Mr. Miyao: This is why we invariably encounter opposition from those who despise people and denigrate the sanctity of life.

President Ikeda: Yes, the Soka Gakkai has faced persecution and slander, precisely because we have continued to strive for justice. Only by triumphing over these obstacles can we truly realize the ideal of "establishing the correct teaching for the peace of the land," and build a world of peace and coexistence through the united efforts of people everywhere.

Mr. Sato: President Ikeda, you battled great obstacles in your youth. On the day when the young men's student division was established (on June 30, 1957), you sent a congratulatory telegram from Hokkaido, where you were in the midst of the human rights struggle known as the Yubari Coal Miners Union Incident [a case of blatant religious discrimination in which miners in Yubari, Hokkaido, were threatened with losing their jobs on account of being Soka Gakkai members]. On that same day, even though you were completely innocent of any crime, you were ordered by the Osaka Prefectural Police to appear for questioning, marking the start of the Osaka Incident.

Mr. Miyao: In the past, the student division representatives of Kansai received these two poems from you:

On this day of release
and of imprisonment are found
the bonds of mentor and disciple.

* * *

Gazing up at Mount Fuji,
I will never forget
July 3.[6]

We will forever make this the fundamental spirit of the student division.

Our Behavior Is Most Important

President Ikeda: It's crucial for you, young revolutionaries striving for justice, to fearlessly forge onward amid the surging waves of life.

Bodhisattva Never Disparaging continued to practice nonviolence, undaunted by arrogant people who looked down on him. His conduct epitomizes utmost respect for others, the noblest conduct as a human being.

Ms. Oyama: So it was through this respectful behavior that he was able to transform the age when the Buddhist Law was about to perish.

President Ikeda: Yes. Nichiren Daishonin writes: "What does Bodhisattva Never Disparaging's profound respect for people signify? The purpose of the appearance in this world of Shakyamuni Buddha, the lord of teachings, lies in his behavior as a human being" (WND-1, 852).

Our humanistic behavior is the most important aspect of our Buddhist practice. It can have a deep, positive impact on the lives of others. The key is always to act with sincerity, to have unwavering commitment and to be in complete earnest. And, above all, it is to have courage. Only through such actions can we genuinely move the hearts of others. By persevering in his practice with sincerity and conviction, Bodhisattva Never Disparaging was able to win ultimate victory.

Mr. Sato: According to the Lotus Sutra, he was able to attain the great benefit of the "purification of the six sense organs" and extend his life span for "two hundred ten thousand million nayutas of years" (LSOC, 309). And, in a later lifetime, he was reborn as Shakyamuni Buddha.

The Daishonin writes, "The people who cursed and struck Bodhisattva Never Disparaging at first behaved with such animosity, but later they took faith in him and became his followers, looking up to him and treating him with great respect" (WND-1, 435). In the end, even those who persecuted Bodhisattva Never Disparaging realized their own error.

President Ikeda: Bodhisattva Never Disparaging triumphed through courage, sincerity and perseverance.

In *The Record of the Orally Transmitted Teachings*, the Daishonin states, "When one faces a mirror and makes a bow of obeisance, the image in the mirror likewise makes a bow of obeisance to oneself" (p. 165). Though the people of overbearing arrogance among the "four kinds of believers"— monks, nuns, laymen and laywomen—persecuted Bodhisattva Never Disparaging, their Buddha nature was actually bowing in reverence to him.

Similarly, when we engage others in dialogue and show respect for their Buddha nature, though they might reject our words at the time, their Buddha nature is in reality venerating our Buddha nature in response. When we sincerely convey the message of Nichiren Buddhism, the seeds of Buddhahood are planted in other people's lives, which begin to move on a course toward positive change.

When we speak out courageously, our Buddha nature is also powerfully manifested. It also activates the innate Buddha nature of the other person. The sincere dialogues we have contribute to our mutual enrichment, happiness and victory.

The only way to actualize kosen-rufu and world peace is in such steadfast efforts in dialogue.

Dialogue Based on Sincere Prayer

Ms. Oyama: Our struggle for kosen-rufu really requires diligent and consistent effort, doesn't it?

President Ikeda: Yes. It's a struggle that requires great perseverance. Yet, these efforts surely but steadily help people transform their lives. This is the power of dialogue in Nichiren Daishonin's "Buddhism of sowing."

The Daishonin writes, "Because I have persevered without fear, there are now people who think my teachings may be true" (WND-1, 489). The dialogues being carried out by you, the youth, are sure to dynamically propel our kosen-rufu movement forward.

Mr. Miyao: We will exert ourselves in dialogue filled with even greater confidence.

President Ikeda: Everyone has the potential for positive change. We mustn't decide that it's useless to talk to someone. If we judge someone's potential like that, it would prove our lack of compassion. To refrain from doing so is the spirit of Bodhisattva Never Disparaging.

Mr. Toda said: "Dialogue based on sincere prayer is infused with the tremendous power of the Buddha," and "If we share Nichiren Buddhism, we can create trust." He also said to the youth: "The powerful life force of one individual can influence and change the lives of others for the better. The surest way of strengthening this inner working of life is the Mystic Law."

Your courageous voices will spread ripples of fresh energy and earn the trust of others.

Mr. Sato: By creating a vibrant groundswell of dialogue for kosen-rufu, we are determined to open the way to victory.

President Ikeda: That's the key to being modern-day Bodhisattvas Never Disparaging.

As I mentioned earlier, Bodhisattva Never Disparaging appeared in an age when the truth that all people's lives are infinitely respectworthy had been lost and society was filled with individuals of overbearing arrogance. It was during such a time that he transformed people's lives through the power of the principle of respect for all human beings.

The noble actions of SGI members today devoting themselves to the happiness of others are in exact accord with those of Bodhisattva Never Disparaging. I hope the youth will emulate the courage of this dedicated bodhisattva.

Our victory in the twenty-first century rests entirely with you, the youth. With the indomitable spirit of Bodhisattva Never Disparaging, please boldly ring in a new age of the triumph of the people.

Notes:

1. George Mason, *The Papers of George Mason,* edited by Robert A. Rutland (Chapel Hill, North Carolina: University of North Carolina Press, 1970), vol. 1, p. 231.

2. The initial stage of rejoicing: Refers to the first of the five stages of practice of the Lotus Sutra formulated by the Great Teacher T'ien-t'ai of China. At this stage, one rejoices on hearing the truth.

3. Translated from Japanese. From an article in the November 8, 1992, *Seikyo Shimbun.*

4. Translated from Japanese. From a lecture delivered at the Institute of Oriental Philosophy, in Hachioji, Tokyo, on November 6, 1992.

5. The Middle Day of the Law here does not refer to the Middle Day after the death of Shakyamuni Buddha, but after the death of Buddha Awesome Sound King. The successive periods of the Former Day, the Middle Day and the Latter Day of the Law were also applied to other Buddhas appearing in Buddhist scriptures. Accordingly, the teaching of each Buddha has its own Middle Day of the Law.

6. On July 3, 1945, second Soka Gakkai president Josei Toda, who had been imprisoned during World War II for opposing Japanese militarism, was released from prison. By strange coincidence, on the same day in 1957, his disciple and successor SGI President Ikeda was arrested and imprisoned by the Osaka Prefectural Police on false charges of violating election laws. July 3 has thus become a day on which tribute is paid to the mystic bonds of mentor and disciple.

Thirteen

Building the Future, Part 1

Soka Gakkai Young Women's Leader Yumiko Kumazawa: President Ikeda, congratulations on receiving an honorary doctorate of humanities from the University of Malaya, in Kuala Lumpur, Malaysia, one of the leading universities in Asia (on August 2, 2010)! The young women's SGI Ikeda Kayo-kai members in Malaysia were overjoyed at this event.

SGI President Ikeda: Thank you. Since the pioneering days of our movement in Malaysia, the members there have made sincere and tireless efforts to contribute to their local communities and society, and have won the trust of their fellow citizens. I share the honor I have received with all of them.

Soka Gakkai Youth Leader Yoshinori Sato: The path of educational and cultural exchange you have opened between Japan and Malaysia is remarkable. So far, more than fifty Soka University students have studied at the University of Malaya. One Soka University graduate has even gone on to earn a doctorate there.

President Ikeda: That's wonderful.

I understand that the pupils at the Malaysia Soka Kindergarten are also developing tremendously. This year (2010) marks the fifteenth anniversary of the kindergarten's opening. In 2000, I personally visited the kindergarten. Living in such an ethnically diverse country, the pupils are

YOUTH AND THE WRITINGS OF NICHIREN DAISHONIN

proud global citizens, playing and learning together harmoniously, their conversations moving freely among Malay, Chinese and English.

You're really missing out if you can only speak one language!

This year also commemorates the eightieth anniversary of Soka education. I'm sure that the first two founding Soka Gakkai presidents, Tsunesaburo Makiguchi and Josei Toda, would be very happy to see how much it has developed.

Soka Gakkai Future Division General Leader Nobutaka Kawamoto: In Japan, summer is a time when we focus on fostering the future division members. [The future division comprises the elementary school division and the junior high and high school divisions.] Leaders across the country are doing everything they can to reach out to and encourage our young members.

Recently, President Ikeda, you took the time to revise the lyrics of the future division song "Seigi no sosha" (Torchbearers of Justice). Young members everywhere are now joyfully singing this song. Thank you very much!

Focus on Making Causes in the Present

President Ikeda: Our future division members are the treasure of the Soka Gakkai, the hope of the world, and the future of humanity. I will do anything to support these young people to whom we will entrust the future of kosen-rufu. If I could, I would like to personally encourage and firmly shake hands with each of them. But since that's simply physically impossible, I'm counting on you, the youth, with your energy and passion, to encourage these young successors on my behalf for they are the very life of the Soka Gakkai.

Mr. Sato: We will do our best. Engraving your spirit in our hearts, we will dedicate ourselves all out to fostering the future division members.

President Ikeda: In "Emergence of the Treasure Tower," the 11th chapter of the Lotus Sutra, Many Treasures Buddha and the Buddhas of the ten directions who are emanations of Shakyamuni gather in the presence of Shakyamuni. Why do they do this? Citing the sutra, Nichiren Daishonin states in "The Opening of the Eyes" that they do so to make certain that the Law will long endure and, more specifically, "to insure the future propagation of the Lotus Sutra so that it can be made available to all the children of the Buddha in times to come" (WND-1, 286).

The focus of the Lotus Sutra, in other words, is the future propagation of the Mystic Law. From the perspective of the Buddha, the main concern is leading "all the children of the Buddha in times to come"—namely, all living beings of the future—to enlightenment. Kosen-rufu is the noble undertaking of "enabling all living beings to attain Buddhahood in the ten thousand years of the Latter Day of the Law" (OTT, 41). Toward that end, it is essential that we foster a steady stream of capable individuals. This is why encouraging a single youth division or future division member serves to create incredible value for the sake of kosen-rufu.

Mr. Kawamoto: The future division is the first division that you established after you were inaugurated as the third Soka Gakkai president (in 1960). Sharing your thoughts on founding the future division, you said: "I am always earnestly thinking about the twenty-first century. Who will take responsibility for kosen-rufu and world peace then? Who will transmit the true Soka Gakkai spirit into the twenty-first century? We can only count on today's future division members."

President Ikeda: I still feel exactly the same way. This is the century in which we must build the foundations for lasting peace and establish the sanctity of life as a universally accepted principle. The SGI has an immense mission to fulfill.

Leading thinkers around the world are increasingly showing understanding for the SGI's dedicated efforts to spiritually enrich people's lives and elevate the life state of humanity as a whole. Today's youth division and future division members have a very important role to play in the world.

Our efforts to foster capable individuals for kosen-rufu are extremely crucial in building the future. As the Daishonin cites from a sutra, "If you want to understand what results will be manifested in the future, look at the causes that exist in the present" (WND-1, 279). What matters are the concrete actions we take now to ensure future victory.

Everyone Is an Entity of the Mystic Law

Ms. Kumazawa: Once, when I attended a meeting as a junior high school division representative, you came up to a group of us, bowed to us respectfully, and said, "I entrust the twenty-first century to you!" This left a powerful impression on me. You treated us as if we were heads of state. I was deeply moved. In that moment, I resolved that I would do my best to develop into a capable person who could contribute to actualizing your vision for kosen-rufu.

President Ikeda: At the assembly described in the Lotus Sutra, it is the eight-year-old dragon king's daughter who demonstrates great actual proof of the enlightenment of women and attaining Buddhahood in one's present form.

Nanjo Tokimitsu was also thought to have been only seven years old when he first met the Daishonin. Later, when he was sixteen, he visited the Daishonin and received instruction from him directly. Tokimitsu was a valiant young champion of the Mystic Law who persevered with courageous faith amid all manner of adversity. The Daishonin praises his unwavering fortitude, writing: "Many people, both high and low, have admonished or threatened you, but you have refused to give up your faith. [You] now appear certain to attain Buddhahood" (WND-1, 1109).

The Mystic Law is a great teaching that enables young people dedicated to the cause of good to shine their brightest. They can freely bring forth the inexhaustible beneficial power of the Mystic Law in the present and the future. I am referring to none other than our future division members. Each of them is a vibrant entity of the Mystic Law.

Mr. Sato: Yes. We should never treat them in a condescending manner just because of their age, but rather advance alongside them as fellow members dedicated to kosen-rufu.

President Ikeda: I'd like to take this opportunity to express my heartfelt appreciation to all the leaders in the youth division, student division, and the men's and women's divisions who are offering guidance and advice to the future division members about life, school and career paths.

Naturally, our future division members are our treasure, but at the same time, those in the elementary school division can be very rowdy, and the junior high and high school division members can also be very emotional. They may not always listen to what you have to say! I know that you, the leaders supporting them, are also occupied with your own family concerns, jobs and other Soka Gakkai activities. I understand what a challenge it is to find the extra time to help and guide the future division members.

In that respect, please always remember: "Where there is unseen virtue, there will be visible reward" (WND-1, 907), and "If one lights a fire for others, one will brighten one's own way" (WND-2, 1060). All the efforts you make to support the future division members will definitely come back to you as great good fortune—the benefit of which will flow on to your children and your descendants into the eternal future.

Mr. Kawamoto: I have heard from some leaders who are supporting the future division members that it can be very challenging when they visit them at their homes as the youngsters often don't open up and aren't really interested in talking about Buddhism. At meetings, some of them just stare down at their feet the whole time.

President Ikeda: I see. That must be trying for both parties concerned!

But isn't it wonderful that these young people are even there? I hope leaders will praise and encourage the future division members for their efforts to come to a meeting. It is often a challenge just for them to attend. No doubt, they would rather be out having fun. The fact is that, in spite of the many other things going on in their lives, they have made it to a meeting. They might not seem enthusiastic about being there or appear to be listening to what people are saying, but in Mr. Toda's words: "Even though they may not change right away, later on, they'll remember they attended a particular meeting. The important thing is that they personally see, hear and experience what goes on at our meetings."

Sometimes, a young person is actually listening carefully, even if they're not looking at the speaker. Sometimes, important words are stored away deep in their hearts.

Mr. Sato: Looking back on my own experience, I can confirm that what you just said is true! With time, I have come to realize how earnestly my leaders were chanting Nam-myoho-renge-kyo for my happiness, and now, I really appreciate their sincere efforts.

President Ikeda: How wonderful it is to experience the realm of Buddhism and form a connection with it! From a long-term perspective, nothing is ever wasted.

In the Daishonin's writings, the story of how King Ashoka came to be an exemplary monarch of peace is mentioned several times. In one letter, he writes, "Long ago, the boy called Virtue Victorious fashioned a mud pie and offered it as alms to Shakyamuni Buddha, and later he [the boy] was reborn as King Ashoka, ruler of Jambudvipa [the entire world], and in the end became a Buddha" (WND-2, 653).

Any action we take for the sake of Buddhism, for our mentor and for kosen-rufu with a youthful, pure-hearted spirit, though it may seem insignificant at the time, will eventually blossom into unimaginable good fortune and benefit. As the Daishonin notes, even a single mud pie, sincerely offered, can lead to one becoming the ruler of the entire world. Though the law of cause and effect in Buddhism is very strict, it also overflows with truly wondrous and fabulous possibilities. The power of the Mystic Law can turn these into reality.

The Daishonin says, "It is the heart that is important" (WND-1, 1000). Through activities to foster the future division in accord with the fundamental principles of Buddhism, we are sowing seeds in young hearts—seeds for developing into great leaders who can achieve outstanding victory and success.

The Soka Gakkai Is a Realm of Happiness

Mr. Kawamoto: When I was in the sixth grade, my mother was hospitalized with cancer. Though my father was busy with work, he did his utmost to take care of us. Still, there were long hours when my two sisters and I were alone at home, and anxiety ate away at us. During that period, many local Soka Gakkai members unhesitatingly came to encourage and support us. They stopped by to visit and chant with us regularly. Sometimes, they even brought us dinner. Eventually, thanks to their support and the encouragement we received from reading your guidance, President Ikeda, my family united as one, and my mother overcame her cancer.

President Ikeda: There is no organization whose members are as dedicated in offering warm support and encouragement as the Soka Gakkai. It is an oasis of human harmony and a haven of happiness. Computers, no matter how advanced, cannot foster human beings. Textbooks alone are not sufficient for developing a sound character. Diamonds can only polish diamonds. Similarly, people are polished and perfected through their interactions with others. This is a universal and enduring truth.

Countless future division and youth division members worldwide have been inspired to stand up as a result of the encouragement of seniors in faith who took the time to reach out and support them. I have received reports from young members in Japan and around the globe expressing their happiness and gratitude to have had such leaders.

Mr. Kawamoto: When I was the elementary school division leader, I met a member who was part of the Saitama Prefecture future division chorus group. His parents had divorced, and he was being bullied at school. Consequently, he spent most of the last half of his junior high school years at home.

A turning point came when, at the persistent invitation of a high school division leader, he attended an open campus event at Soka University in Hachioji, Tokyo. He was moved by the warm welcome he received at the university, and it prompted him to recall the pledge he had made to himself when he was younger to someday attend Soka University. He began to study really hard and eventually gained acceptance to Soka University.

During his freshman year, President Ikeda, you unexpectedly visited his classroom and, much to his surprise, sat right next him to listen to the law lecture being given. Now, always cherishing the encouragement you gave him at that time, he is applying himself earnestly to his graduate studies.

President Ikeda: Yes, he's kept me well updated on his activities. He has grown into a fine young man.

It is all of you, the members of today's future and youth divisions, who will be key in ensuring that we celebrate the Soka Gakkai's one hundredth anniversary in 2030 with resounding victory. You are also the ones who will ring in a new series of Seven Bells—symbolizing the development of our movement unfolding over seven seven-year periods, beginning from May 3, 2001—and bring it to a triumphant culmination in 2050.

The Daishonin writes, "All the various teachings of the Buddha are spread by persons" (WND-1, 61). No matter how wonderful the teaching we uphold or how grand our buildings, if we do not continue to produce a steady stream of capable individuals to carry on our work, the great flow of kosen-rufu will come to a halt. Mr. Toda once said: "People are what matter. Everything depends on people. Everything depends on each individual youth."

In "On the Buddha's Prophecy," the Daishonin writes: "Even when [in more recent times] . . . priests set out from Japan to take some sutras [back] to China, no one was found there who could embrace these sutras and teach them to others. It was as though there were only wooden or stone statues garbed in priests' robes and carrying begging bowls" (WND-1, 401). In other words, he is saying that there were no successors. Any organization will perish without successors. The only way to ensure that the correct teaching of Buddhism endures is to foster a constant stream of capable individuals who genuinely embrace and practice it.

Sincerity, Passion and Genuineness Are the Key

Mr. Sato: President Ikeda, you recognized early on the problems that would be caused by declining birthrates in Japan. Regarding that issue, you said: "In an age of declining birthrates, each person is of utmost importance and must be wholeheartedly treasured. If each individual is fostered into a person of outstanding ability, a peaceful future will be assured." We are determined to treasure each person even more than we have been.

President Ikeda: Sincerity, passion and genuineness are the key. Earnestly chant to foster successors who will surpass you. Children notice a leader's spirit, dedication and way of life. From the time I was a young man, I have taken every opportunity to encourage the children of Soka Gakkai members. Whenever I attended a meeting at a private home, I would always thank the family who lived there and also make a point of talking to their children, as well.

Ms. Kumazawa: Mrs. Ikeda can be considered one of the very first future division members. As a young girl, she once accompanied President Makiguchi from the nearest train station to her family's home for a discussion meeting. Later, when she was in the young women's division, she looked after the children that mothers brought with them to meetings, reading them stories and encouraging them. She is truly among the first to take responsibility for caring for future division members.

President Ikeda: Mr. Toda declared: "Children are the treasures of the future. Think of them as emissaries from the future, and take the best care of them."

My wife and I have simply always acted in accord with this guidance.

Mr. Kawamoto: Emeritus Professor Akira Morishima of Joetsu University of Education has praised the Soka Gakkai's tradition of fostering young people. He noted how valuable it is to have youth in their twenties and thirties interacting with boys and girls who are still in the process of completing their school studies, sharing advice and acting as older brothers and sisters to them.

President Ikeda: Many thinking people are aware of the positive things we are doing. In today's dog-eat-dog world, our movement, with its sincere commitment to treasuring the younger generation, shines ever more brightly as a source of hope.

Mr. Sato: It has been fifteen years since you established the Twenty-first Century Mission Group, which comprises youth leaders responsible for raising the future division. You have said to the members of this group, "All of you, who are fostering the leaders of kosen-rufu for the twenty-first century, possess an unsurpassed mission and are making an invaluable contribution to our movement."

President Ikeda: Those who foster capable people are truly capable themselves. The warm light of the sun is a source of life and growth. The sun is a symbol of hope, courage and compassion. I would like all of you, the leaders of the future division, to exert yourselves even more energetically and shine as suns that brighten and illuminate the lives of our young members.

I know how busy you are and how things might not always go as smoothly as you would like. But the sun always rises serenely and unperturbedly, no matter what happens. In the same way, please continue on the path of your mission with firm resolve and purpose.

The Daishonin writes, "The Lotus Sutra is [like] the sun" (see WND-1, 315). May you always strive to bring forth in your heart a bright, invincible, ever-victorious sun.

Fourteen

Building the Future, Part 2

Soka Gakkai Young Women's Division Leader Yumiko Kumazawa: Many future division members have grown tremendously due to the warm encouragement of various leaders. I myself experienced a significant turning point when I was in my third year of junior high school. I planned to take the entrance examination for Soka High School, but was having a difficult time with my studies. At the point when I was considering throwing in the towel, a leader encouraged me, saying that I shouldn't give up as long as there was still the slightest possibility that I could get in. Her words inspired me to study even harder. I'm deeply grateful to her to this day.

SGI President Ikeda: There are many people behind the scenes who have encouraged and supported young people in taking entrance examinations and gaining acceptance into the Soka schools and Soka University. As the founder of those institutions, I'd like to express my heartfelt gratitude to them all.

A single word of encouragement can be a tremendous driving force for young, developing lives. Nichiren Daishonin writes, "Teaching another something is the same as oiling the wheels of a cart so that they turn even though it is heavy, or as floating a boat on water so that it moves ahead easily" (WND-1, 1086). It is important to encourage future division members in a way that enables them to move forward and demonstrate their full potential. We need to empower them and help lighten and brighten their hearts.

Even if you can't meet with them in person, a single phone call can help them break through something that may be holding them back. Sometimes even writing an encouraging note can be all it takes to change a person's life.

Soka Gakkai Future Division General Leader Nobutaka Kawamoto: Members who are trying to get into a high school or university are facing an especially crucial time in their lives. Warm encouragement from their youth division leaders, as well as their families, is really important.

President Ikeda: Students studying for entrance exams are dealing with much more pressure and anxiety than adults are often aware of. The eminent British historian Arnold Toynbee (1889–1975) recalled that once, when he was faced with crushing exam pressures, his parents' words really encouraged him. They told him: "Just do your best . . . None of us can do more than that."[1] I ask that you, the leaders of the youth division, encourage the future division so that they freely bring forth their full potential.

Learning Broadens Your Perspective

Soka Gakkai Youth Division Leader Yoshinori Sato: President Ikeda, you studied at "Toda University" and have now received academic honors from 295 institutions of higher learning around the world.[2] This is an unprecedented achievement. We, in turn, are proud to be students of "Ikeda University," and learning from you what matters most.

The youth of Soka will carry on in your footsteps and build a leading network of wisdom and learning.

President Ikeda: Learning is light—that was the spirit of founding Soka Gakkai president Tsunesaburo Makiguchi and his successor Josei Toda, both great educators.

Presently, amid the hot summer season here in Japan, summer in-class sessions for the Soka University Division of Correspondence Education are taking place at Soka University. Correspondence students, many of whom have come from overseas, are giving their all to their studies, setting a noble example of dedication to learning.

Especially for the future division members, the opportunity to study is a precious right and privilege. Learning broadens your perspective and expands the arena of possibilities in your lives. It enables you to see the world in ways you have never seen before. It effectively gives you wings to soar high into the sky and gain a broad vantage of the world.

That is why I would like you to study as hard as you can at this stage in your lives. Read good books. And if you can, go to a university.

Mr. Sato: I know many future division members who have resolved to go to a university after a leader shared with them how they were unable to receive a higher education themselves and that they hoped the future division members would go in their stead.

President Ikeda: That's very admirable. The encouragement of those leaders embodies the ideals of humanistic education. At the age of twelve, Nichiren Daishonin vowed to become "the wisest person in all Japan" (WND-1, 175). This vow is the starting point of Nichiren Buddhism. The future division's proud tradition of placing top priority on study and learning is directly connected to the Daishonin's spirit.

In *The Record of the Orally Transmitted Teachings*, the Daishonin is quoted as saying, "It is due to the authority and supernatural power of Bodhisattva Universal Worthy that this Lotus Sutra is propagated throughout Jambudvipa [the entire world]" (p. 190). Leaders who embrace universal wisdom, as represented by Bodhisattva Universal Worthy, will be on the forefront of the movement for worldwide kosen-rufu.

The growth and development of our future division members today will spread hope for humanity tomorrow.

Ms. Kumazawa: Yes. And we, as their leaders, should enthusiastically study together with them and demonstrate the wisdom of Buddhism in society. The problems children face today are becoming increasingly complex and challenging, including bullying, absence from school and social withdrawal.

President Ikeda: In his *Soka kyoikugaku taikei* (The System of Value-Creating Education), which was published eighty years ago, Mr. Makiguchi wrote to the effect: "I am driven by the frantic desire to prevent the present deplorable situation, where ten million of our children and students are forced to endure the agonies of cutthroat competition . . . from continuing into the next generation. Therefore, I have no time to be concerned with the shifting vagaries of public opinion."

Embracing this spirit as their own, the members of the Soka Gakkai Education Department are striving with tireless commitment on the front lines of education. Today, as a department, they have compiled more than forty thousand educational field reports from schoolteachers on overcoming various problems and challenges faced by them or their students.

Moreover, the Education Counseling Program that is run at some Soka Gakkai culture centers throughout the country and the Retired Educators Group are both shining examples of reliable educational resources for the community.

For the sake of the happiness of our children, it is important not just for schools but also families, local communities and societies to put even greater effort into improving education. American futurist Hazel Henderson has said, "Of course, education is absolutely vital; but in society as a whole we must revive love and passion for serving our children."[3] The realm of the Soka Gakkai family, in which districts and chapters are united in watching over and fostering our children, is a pioneering example of this.

Advance—Even If It's Only One or Two Inches!

Mr. Kawamoto: That is very true. I recently heard a joint experience by a mother and her son about how they overcame the son's refusal to attend school for five years. The son had become withdrawn and wouldn't talk for days on end. However, the mother, inspired by your words that "night always turns into day" and the warm encouragement of seniors in faith, summoned the courage to challenge this situation. She chanted Nam-myoho-renge-kyo earnestly and gave her all to participating in Soka Gakkai activities.

Every evening, the mother would tell her son about what she had done that day. Eventually, he began to communicate haltingly, until a smile finally returned to his face. In the end, he shared with his mother that he wanted to go to a university. He was able to realize his dream, and is now pursuing graduate studies at Soka University.

In his experience, the son shared a passage he had read from your dialogue *Discussions on Youth* that had struck a chord with him: "The important thing is to keep pressing forward. While struggling with various problems, it is vital that you chant Nam-myoho-renge-kyo and advance somehow—even if it's only one or two inches. If you do so, when you look back, you'll see that you have actually made your way through the jungle in no time."[4]

President Ikeda: Yes, I have heard about their experience. When things looked bleakest, the mother resolved that she would absolutely surmount this difficulty and use what she had learned to encourage others struggling with similar problems. That is what enabled her to be so strong. And now, she has become a key figure in her community, encouraging other mothers. This is an example of the way of life of changing karma into mission, based on the Buddhist principle that we "voluntarily take on the appropriate karma."

Every family has their own unique set of problems, such as financial hardship and illness. Referring to these kinds of challenges, the Daishonin says, "Probably the ten demon daughters are testing the strength of your faith" (WND-1, 899).

Never be afraid, no matter how daunting the problem seems. Just say to yourself that your faith is being put to the test and rise up to face the difficulty courageously. If you do that, you will definitely "change poison into medicine," and elevate and expand your life state in the process.

Mr. Sato: Soka Gakkai families have countless golden experiences of this kind. It is important that we tell our friends and fellow members about the wonderful benefits we receive through our practice.

President Ikeda: We are living in a time when people are increasingly seeking the teachings of Buddhism. The Daishonin writes, "Teach others to the best of your ability, even if it is only a single sentence or phrase" (WND-1, 386). I would like our youth division members to brim with strong conviction as they create a dynamic groundswell that will further expand our movement for kosen-rufu.

Ms. Kumazawa: You can count on us. We, the members of the Ikeda Kayo-kai, are confidently telling our friends about this wonderful path that enables us to enjoy a truly fulfilling youth and happy, value-filled lives.

Mr. Sato: In an age when there are so many negative influences, the dialogues we are sharing with others are creating good, positive influences.

We are now seeing a rise in cases of young people falling victim to cyber crime—crime perpetrated through cell phones, computers and the Internet. I think it is important for us to warn our precious members of the future and youth divisions about these dangers to keep them safe from harm.

President Ikeda: The Daishonin said that in this evil age of the Latter Day of the Law, people's hearts would become "as bestial as dogs or tigers" (WND-1, 325). We see especially vicious crimes and incidents occurring today that years ago wouldn't have been imagined possible. It is important for communities and families to make children aware of these things. We need to "be even more careful than usual" (WND-2, 731). Lack of vigilance can have terrible results. Earnest daily recitation of the sutra and chanting Nam-myoho-renge-kyo are the foundation.

Start by Listening

Mr. Kawamoto: Some future division leaders say that when they deal with the members, they can't help but feel a generation gap.

President Ikeda: I see. But remember, when you were in the future division, your leaders probably said the very same thing about you! The fact of the matter is, your being of a different generation means that you have something special to share with younger people. In school, they generally interact only with friends of the same age. That is what makes perspective and advice from someone who has experience in the real world and a broader view of life so valuable to them. Your perspective is very meaningful, in both educational and social terms. Listen carefully to what they have to say, as good older brothers and sisters. The first step is to reach out to them and make friends. You don't have to make it complicated. Buddhism teaches us just to be ourselves. Just share with the youth your honest enthusiasm about working for kosen-rufu.

Mr. Sato: Dr. Vincent Harding, with whom you are presently engaged in a dialogue, has said something similar. At times, he noted, adults and teachers may be experiencing feelings of disappointment and frustration when interacting with children, but that, too, can be a good educational opportunity, because it shows children how adults deal with those feelings.[5]

President Ikeda: Children are truly keen observers. Like young trees reaching up toward the sky, they seek out the warm sun of hope. They thirst for rich nourishment for their hearts and minds. Children have the ability to absorb things like a sponge. They develop and grow rapidly.

As I mentioned before, the Daishonin encouraged his young follower Nanjo Tokimitsu repeatedly, from the time Tokimitsu was the age of some of today's future division members. Out of his wish to see the young man grow into a fine adult, like a loving father, the Daishonin instructed and guided Tokimitsu, who had lost his actual father when he was a boy.

Ms. Kumazawa: There are more than thirty letters in the Daishonin's collected writings that are addressed to Nanjo Tokimitsu.

President Ikeda: Each of them offers timeless lessons for future division members. For example, the Daishonin gives detailed advice about how to behave toward one's parents. A good son or daughter, he says, "is always mindful of providing a parent with all manner of good things, and if this happens to be impossible, in the course of a day one at least smiles twice or thrice in their direction" (WND-2, 636). Just a smile from their child is enough to make a parent happy!

Mr. Kawamoto: Being good sons and daughters to our parents, which you've emphasized repeatedly, has become a motto for future division members.

Become Leaders of Integrity

President Ikeda: Because of his high aspirations in the future for Tokimitsu, the Daishonin strictly instructed him in the importance of maintaining a correct attitude in faith. In a letter written to a teenage Tokimitsu, the Daishonin lists the names of those who had abandoned their faith or betrayed their mentor, warning the young man of the consequences of turning against one's teacher or disrupting the harmonious community of believers.

He says: "Sho-bo, Noto-bo and the lay nun of Nagoe were once Nichiren's disciples. Greedy, cowardly, and foolish, they nonetheless pass themselves off as wise persons. When persecutions befell me, they took advantage of these to convince many of my followers to drop out" (WND-1, 800).

In other words, these individuals had allowed themselves to be defeated by greed, cowardice, ignorance and arrogance.

The Daishonin clearly instilled a sense of truth and justice in the life of his young successor. Following the Daishonin's guidance, Tokimitsu grew up to be a leader of staunch integrity who fought against evil and resolutely protected his fellow practitioners. When disciples courageously stand up for the same noble cause as their mentor, the way to the eternal transmission of the Mystic Law is opened.

Ms. Kumazawa: There is nothing more wonderful than knowing our mentor is watching over our long-term growth. You wrote the following message to the young men and young women of the high school division Young Phoenix training groups on receiving a collection of their determinations in the summer of 1991, in commemoration of the twenty-fifth anniversary of the groups' establishment:

Eternal cheers
for the Young Phoenix groups
as you raise high the banner of victory.
Hurrah!
With palms pressed together in reverence.

Courageous individuals
who are giving your all for the sake of
the Soka Gakkai and your fellow members,
as people committed to truth and justice,
you are true champions who will enjoy
happiness and victory throughout the three existences.

Beneath those words, you drew an image of many phoenixes in flight.

President Ikeda: Fostering people means continuing to pray for and encourage them. It means watching over their brilliant endeavors as they develop and grow into fine individuals. Nothing is more joyful or rewarding.

Personal Growth Is the Foundation

Mr. Sato: An important topic during this year's Future Division Dynamic Growth Month (in August) was passing down faith in the family. Sometimes when we have discussions with members who have children in the future division, we are asked about how to share Buddhism with the younger generation.

President Ikeda: I once shared the following guidelines for parents regarding practicing Nichiren Buddhism within the family:

1. Remember that faith is for a lifetime, but the main focus for your children right now is their studies.
2. Find ways each day to communicate and interact with your children.
3. Refrain from arguing in front of your children.
4. Refrain from both scolding your children at the same time.
5. Be fair and don't compare your children to others.
6. Convey to your children through your example the beliefs and convictions that guide your life.

Each child has unlimited inner potential. They have a rich and unique personality. Cheerfully impart self-confidence to them and nurture their growth by praising them.

The only way for parents to pass on Buddhist faith and practice to their children is to demonstrate their own development through faith. Show your children how great and wonderful this practice and the Soka Gakkai are through your own vibrant and inspiring example.

Mr. Toda said that we should inspire children with our own ideals. Talk to them about your beliefs, about the things you care about. There is no more wonderful gift a parent can give to a child.

Celebrating the birth of a follower's child, the Daishonin writes, "Now you have been blessed with this daughter . . . who can act as a filial child, carrying on your line in this present existence, and in your next existence guiding you to the attainment of Buddhahood" (WND-2, 457).

In the Soka Gakkai family, members should treat all future division members as precious treasures, just as if they were their own children. When the one hundredth anniversary of the Soka Gakkai comes in 2030, the present future division members will be fine young leaders. No doubt they will look back and express their gratitude to their seniors in faith who encouraged them when they were children, and with a deep sense of gratitude, they will support and foster the future division members of that time. A relay of people who "inherit the soul of the Lotus Sutra" (WND-1, 839) will be established, from one generation of Bodhisattvas of the Earth to the next.

As long as the noble spirit of the "oneness of mentor and disciple" continues to be passed on, the Soka Gakkai will flourish for thousands of years to come, and the flame of kosen-rufu will burn for all eternity.

I would like to say once again to future division members and all youth division members, the torchbearers of justice and flag bearers of victory: I entrust the Soka Gakkai of the twenty-first century to you!

Notes:

1. Arnold Toynbee, *Experiences* (New York: Oxford University Press, 1969), p. 6.

2. As of October 2012, SGI President Ikeda has received academic honors from 332 institutions of higher learning around the world.

3. Hazel Henderson and Daisaku Ikeda, *Planetary Citizenship: Your Values, Beliefs, and Actions Can Shape a Sustainable World* (Santa Monica, California: Middleway Press, 2004), p. 149.

4. Daisaku Ikeda, *Discussions on Youth* (Santa Monica, California: World Tribune Press, 2010), p. 5.

5. Translated from Japanese. From an article from the March 1, 2011, *Seikyo Shimbun*.

Fifteen

The Soka Network: An Alliance of People Dedicated to Good, Part 1

Soka Gakkai Young Men's Leader Nobuhisa Tanano: This October (2010) marks fifty years since you first visited the U.N. Headquarters in New York and declared that the twenty-first century would be the "Century of Africa." We would like to express our wholehearted congratulations to you on receiving the Commander of the Order of Merit of Côte d'Ivoire in this significant year. The award is a source of great joy for all SGI members.

SGI President Ikeda: Since mentor and disciple are one and inseparable, I would like to humbly dedicate the award to first and second Soka Gakkai presidents Tsunesaburo Makiguchi and Josei Toda. All of the awards I have received are proof of the support and praise of people around the world for our movement of peace, culture and education.

In Côte d'Ivoire today, more than twenty thousand SGI members, uniting around General Director André Déason, are playing active roles in society as model citizens. And particularly conspicuous are the valiant efforts of the youth division members.

My wish is to pass on and entrust to you, my youthful successors, the great Soka path of mission and glory.

What prompted me to say fifty years ago that the twenty-first century would be the "Century of Africa"? It was the sight of new nations declaring independence one after another in a continent that had experienced great oppression and suffering. Young leaders were courageously rising up and beginning to rebuild their countries with fresh vigor and hope.

Youth have unlimited power. Especially those who uphold a sound philosophy in the days of their youth are invincible.

Soka Gakkai Young Women's Leader Yumiko Kumazawa: SGI members are now joyfully and energetically practicing Nichiren Buddhism in some forty countries and territories in Africa. Even in Sierra Leone, where a civil war lasted for more than a decade (1991–2002), SGI members, under the leadership of a bright young woman, are actively holding discussion meetings and spreading waves of dialogue for peace.

Youth Are Sharing Buddhism To Overcome the Desolation of the Spirit

President Ikeda: Côte d'Ivoire's first president Félix Houphouët-Boigny (1905–93) stated, "Dialogue is the arm of the strong, not the weak."[1]

The courageous dialogues that you of the youth division are carrying out can have a profound impact on others. Throughout the Soka Gakkai's history, youth have always taken the lead in our movement. When youth rally other youth, they can create a groundswell of energy that ushers in a new age.

I hope all of you, the youth of Japan, will also make your best efforts.

Mr. Tanano: Yes, we will do our best!

I feel that we are living in uncertain times. People often keep in touch with others superficially, through cell phones and email, but rarely do they talk with them heart to heart. But, we, the youth of the Soka Gakkai, are very fortunate in that we have clear direction for the future gained from you, President Ikeda, and that we have fellow members on whom we can count for support and encouragement.

Currently, the youth division members in Japan are actively reaching out to others in dialogue to introduce them to Nichiren Buddhism. As a result of these efforts, many young people have expressed their wish to join the Soka Gakkai.

President Ikeda: I'm very happy to hear that. Your actions accord with the passage from Nichiren Daishonin's writings: "At first only Nichiren chanted Nam-myoho-renge-kyo, but then two, three, and a hundred followed, chanting and teaching others. Propagation will unfold this way in the future as well. Does this not signify 'emerging from the earth'?" (WND-1, 385). The Daishonin would surely be delighted to see your achievements.

I believe all young people, in the depths of their hearts, seek a solid philosophy that can guide them in realizing their true potential. I felt the same way in my youth during the turbulent years following World War II. Many young people like myself saw the attitude of the older generations who did a complete about-turn—from an avid support of the war to a sudden professed allegiance to peace and democracy—and this left us with a deep-seated distrust of older people.

But many of us still kept on seeking a philosophy that we could truly put our faith in. Fortunately, I was able to meet Mr. Toda and learn about Nichiren Buddhism and its teaching of the sanctity of life. Because I was thirsting for a worthy philosophy, I was overjoyed when I encountered it. Many of the youth who joined the Soka Gakkai during this period felt the same way. This joy is what built the youthful Soka Gakkai that subsequently emerged.

Mr. Tanano: Many people today feel a spiritual desolation—an emptiness and lack of direction—that perhaps resembles the situation in postwar Japan. The employment conditions are bleak, and young people are searching for a genuinely meaningful and fulfilling way of life. I think this is precisely why the youth division's efforts to share Nichiren Buddhism have profound significance in society, too.

President Ikeda: I agree. People today seem more isolated and disconnected, and human ties are increasingly growing weaker.

Human beings need one another to survive. No matter how tough one tries to act in being alone, a lonely life is sad and unhappy. It doesn't bring a true sense of happiness.

If the number of isolated youth increases, society, too, will invariably face many problems. Now, more than ever, a philosophy that unites people and dialogue that forges heart-to-heart connections are essential for leading truly rich and fulfilling lives.

Our Lives Are Precious Treasures

Ms. Kumazawa: Recently, I was asked a question by a young women's division member. She said, "What is the aim of the dialogue we in the Soka Gakkai carry out?" I thought this question might be related to what we have been discussing.

Mr. Tanano: The immediate response that comes to mind is "kosen-rufu."

President Ikeda: That's true, of course, but I think she's after a more specific answer.

This is an important question. To explain from one perspective, I think we can say that our efforts for dialogue aim to deepen and broaden the bonds among people. This could be called, I suppose, an expansion of an alliance of people dedicated to good.

In *The Record of the Orally Transmitted Teachings*, the Daishonin states: "'Joy' means that oneself and others together experience joy . . . Both oneself and others together will take joy in their possession of wisdom and compassion" (p. 146).

What is the aim of our dialogues? It is to manifest our Buddha nature and help others do the same. In other words, it is to reveal the supreme good within us that shines with wisdom and compassion.

Ms. Kumazawa: What you just mentioned reminds me of the discussion you had with youth representatives on the respectful behavior of Bodhisattva Never Disparaging (see pp. 125–36). Isn't the ultimate point of our dialogues to revive a philosophy of respect for all people and create an age in which all life is honored?

President Ikeda: That's correct. But if this were a simple task, we wouldn't have to strive so hard.

The Lotus Sutra describes the wisdom of the Buddha as "difficult to believe and difficult to understand" (LSOC, 173). Most people can't believe that they inherently possess the noble life state of Buddhahood within them. They don't realize that their own life is a precious treasure with infinite potential.

While there are some people who put themselves down, there are also others who look down on others, thinking arrogantly that they are special, and unable to believe that all people are equally respectworthy. I'm sure many of you in the youth division have had experiences in which you shared Nichiren Buddhism with others, but they just didn't seem to understand it.

Ultimately, the dialogues we in the Soka Gakkai undertake are a struggle against the devilish functions within life that create unhappiness and division, a struggle against the delusion or ignorance that gives rise to mistrust and hatred.

The Daishonin writes of the intensity of this struggle, "The devil king of the sixth heaven has roused the ten kinds of troops and, in the midst of the sea of the sufferings of birth and death, is at war with the votary of the Lotus Sutra to stop him from taking possession of and to wrest away from him this impure land where both ordinary people and sages dwell" (WND-2, 465).

Sharing Nichiren Buddhism, expanding friendship, doing home visits—each is an expression of respect for others' Buddha nature. In our society where egoism and mistrust seem to abound, a gathering like the Soka Gakkai that believes in and takes action for others to this extent is surely difficult to find.

The Seeds of Buddhahood Will Blossom Without Fail

Mr. Tanano: The peace activist Arun Gandhi, who carries on the legacy of his grandfather, Mahatma Gandhi (1869–1948), has declared, "To become someone who can respect others as equal human beings—only by this change of attitude gradually taking place in each person's life can we positively transform society and the world."[2] He also commented that the SGI's movement for human revolution is a way of actualizing this, and it is therefore a source of great hope.

Even in challenging circumstances where most people would give up, our seniors in faith have persevered in dialogue and opened the way forward.

President Ikeda: The Daishonin states: "The Buddha is also called 'One Who Can Endure'" (WND-1, 41), and "This mind of forbearance is called Shakyamuni Buddha" (OTT, 169). Soka Gakkai members have embodied these golden words in a time that is described in the sutras as the evil age of the Latter Day of the Law.

We continue to share Nichiren Buddhism with others, even if at first they may react negatively, because we believe in their inherent Buddha nature. Fundamentally, by doing so, we are expressing our deep respect for them.

Sharing Nichiren Buddhism with others is a way to expand both our own life and that of others. The more efforts we make toward this end, the more we awaken and activate other people's Buddha nature, while

166

simultaneously strengthening our own Buddha nature.

The Daishonin writes, "Because one has heard the Lotus Sutra, which leads to Buddhahood, with this as the seed, one will invariably become a Buddha" (WND-1, 882). By introducing others to Nichiren Buddhism, we plant the seeds of Buddhahood in their lives—seeds that will definitely come to bloom in the future.

Mr. Tanano: There was a time when I traveled from Tokyo to my friend's house in Osaka almost every week for six months, to talk with him about Nichiren Buddhism. Even though I chanted wholeheartedly and engaged him in dialogue, he still did not show any interest in practicing. I felt really discouraged.

But, to my surprise, my friend's mother had overheard our conversation from the room next door. And she asked my mother, who had been telling her about Nichiren Buddhism for a long time, if she could join the Soka Gakkai.

Ten years later, my long-standing prayer was finally realized, and my friend also received the Gohonzon. Through this experience, I learned the importance of believing in others to the very end. Since then, my friendship with him has become even closer.

President Ikeda: That's a wonderful experience.

The earnest words of a young man can deeply move others' hearts. A young woman's smile can open closed hearts. A young student's passion and sincerity can rouse others to action. Everyone possesses within their life the incredible potential to touch people's lives through dialogue.

In the Lotus Sutra, the Bodhisattvas of the Earth are described as "clever at difficult questions and answers, their minds know[ing] no fear" (LSOC, 263). All of you, youthful Bodhisattvas of the Earth, have appeared in this defiled age with the ability to surmount obstacles and pioneer new paths for the sake of realizing kosen-rufu.

Everything starts with courage. For us ordinary beings, courage substitutes for compassion. We show compassion to others by having the courage to speak with them. Steadfast dialogue is a sure way of doing good. It is a path of spreading happiness. And it leads to a magnificent revival of the human spirit, elevating the life state of humankind and connecting the hearts of people everywhere.

Openhearted Dialogue Arises From Belief in Others

Ms. Kumazawa: President Ikeda, through your efforts in dialogue and your humanistic actions, you have expanded our network of friendship and peace around the globe. Nearly four decades ago, during the Cold War, you made your first visits to China and the Soviet Union (in 1974) amid intense opposition from both inside and outside the organization.

President Ikeda: At that time, people in Japan immediately reacted with fear when they heard of the Soviet Union. But I decided to go there to have dialogue, because I was convinced that it was not the Soviet Union that was frightening, but our own ignorance.

Mr. Tanano: When you first met with Mikhail Gorbachev, former president of the Soviet Union, at the Kremlin in Moscow (in July 1990), you said to him, "Today, I've come to have an argument with you." For a moment, President Gorbachev's interpreter hesitated to convey your remarks.

You continued, "Let's make sparks fly and talk about everything honestly and openly, for the sake of humanity, and for the sake of Japan and the Soviet Union!" The meeting that began with your call to have frank and openhearted dialogue ended in President Gorbachev stating his intention to visit Japan. He fulfilled this promise the following spring (in April 1991), marking the first visit to Japan by a Soviet head of state.

Ms. Kumazawa: Learning from the brilliant example of citizen diplomacy that you and Mrs. Ikeda have set for us, we of the young women's division are determined to nurture friendship and hope through dialogue in our respective places of mission.

President Ikeda: Viewed from the life philosophy of Nichiren Buddhism, all people regardless of nationality or ethnicity are entities of the "mutual possession of the Ten Worlds" and "three thousand realms in a single moment of life."

As human beings, we all essentially desire for happiness and peace. This conviction is our fundamental spirit.

Developing Ourselves Through Adversity

Mr. Tanano: Many youth today struggle with human relationships in the workplace. Some are unable to get along harmoniously with co-workers, avoiding personal connections with them, while others quickly become emotional and often find themselves in conflicts.

President Ikeda: I'm sure this can be looked at in many different ways, but I think at the root of such problems lies a mistrust toward others on the one hand and a lack of self-confidence on the other. Of course, it may also be related to the times we live in.

The Daishonin writes, "The extremity of greed, anger, and foolishness in people's hearts in the impure world of the latter age makes it difficult for any worthy or sage to control" (WND-1, 1121). The Latter Day is an age in which people's minds are confused and impure. Furthermore, it is an age when society is unstable and deadlocked, and conflict between people is rife. This is precisely why we need a solid philosophy on which we can base our lives.

Shijo Kingo, one of the Daishonin's followers, also struggled in his workplace. He encountered opposition as a result of sharing Nichiren Buddhism with his lord and was the target of slanderous rumors by jealous colleagues. Many around him harbored malice and resentment toward him.

However, the Daishonin writes to the embattled Shijo Kingo, "A fire burns higher when logs are added, and a strong wind makes a kalakula grow larger" (WND-1, 471). A *kalakula* is a mythological insect that is said to grow larger when a strong wind blows. Here, the Daishonin is encouraging his disciple that the harsher the winds of adversity blow, the more he will be able to develop himself and strengthen his faith.

Complaining won't get us anywhere. Faith in Nichiren Buddhism is the driving force for doing our human revolution and becoming stronger and wiser. Our practice enables us to transform even the negative relationships in our lives that cause us suffering into positive relationships that help us grow.

Chanting With the Shared Commitment of Mentor and Disciple Is the Key to Victory

Mr. Tanano: In another letter, the Daishonin also warns Shijo Kingo against his impulsive nature, saying, "You are hot-tempered and behave like a blazing fire" (WND-1, 839).

President Ikeda: Shijo Kingo was forthright and honest, but he was also short-tempered. In the passage you have cited, the Daishonin is advising him not to unnecessarily antagonize his colleagues and friends through such behavior.

When we read Nichiren Daishonin's writings, we can clearly see that he firmly grasped the personality and situation of each of his disciples and offered them surprisingly detailed guidance.

The Daishonin also instructs Shijo Kingo that no matter how trying his circumstances, he "must act and speak without the least servility"

(WND-1, 824). As people who are committed to truth and justice, it's important for us, too, to always stand proud no matter what happens. If we become timid and servile, it will allow injustice to run rampant and devilish functions to take control. And if that were to happen, not only would we be unable to protect our fellow members, but we would do a great disservice to our mentor. That's why it's crucial for us to confidently rise to action as disciples. When we firmly determine to win for the sake of realizing our mentor's vision and for the happiness of fellow members, we'll be able to tap boundless power from within.

Ms. Kumazawa: Shijo Kingo, who was also a skilled physician, later regained his lord's trust by successfully treating his illness. He emerged triumphant in the end, having his land increased threefold.

President Ikeda: The key to his victory was his prayer with the same spirit as his mentor, and his courageous and sincere behavior.

The Daishonin writes, "Bring forth the great power of faith, and be spoken of by all the people of Kamakura, both high and low, or by all the people of Japan, as 'Shijo Kingo, Shijo Kingo of the Lotus school!' " (WND-1, 319). This passage is an eternal guideline for all of us. Our members everywhere have always engraved these words in their hearts and continued to strive with great perseverance. That's why we are strong.

We have entered an age in which all of you, a noble gathering of Soka youth who uphold the sound philosophy of Nichiren Buddhism, will shine ever more brilliantly. The light of your human revolution will brighten your communities, your workplaces and your societies.

Indeed, all the members of our Soka network, an alliance of people dedicated to good, will transform the destiny of their nations and, further, the future of humankind.

People the world over are eagerly awaiting your dynamic development.

Notes:

1. From a speech delivered at the annual greetings to the Diplomatic Corps, on January 1, 1970.

2. Translated from Japanese. From an article in the January 1, 2000, *Seikyo Shimbun*.

─────── Sixteen ───────

The Soka Network:
An Alliance of People
Dedicated to Good, Part 2

SGI President Ikeda: First, please allow me to express my sincere condolences to all those who were affected by the recent rain storms in Amami Oshima [in Kagoshima Prefecture, Kyushu Region]. I am praying wholeheartedly for their speediest possible recovery from the deluge.

Soka Gakkai Young Men's Leader Nobuhisa Tanano: Many of the Kyushu youth division members, together with the men's and women's division members, are actively involved in relief and recovery efforts. I've heard that the Amami members are also valiantly rising up to the challenge, taking to heart the message of encouragement you sent them.

President Ikeda: All our noble Amami members are lions. In the past, even in the face of indescribable hardships, they transformed poison into medicine with the spirit of a lion king. I am praying with all my might that this time, too, the members living on the beautiful island of Amami Oshima will be ever more triumphant and prosperous. For as Nichiren Daishonin states: "Though calamities may come, they can be changed into good fortune" (WND-2, 669), and "When great evil occurs, great good follows" (WND-1, 1119).

Soka Gakkai Young Women's Leader Yumiko Kumazawa: No matter what trials they have encountered, the women's division members in Amami have always emerged victorious with the motto "Let's keep fighting as long as we live!"

President Ikeda: In a letter to Nichinyo, one of his female disciples, the Daishonin writes: "A woman who makes offerings to [this] Gohonzon invites happiness in this life, and in the next, the Gohonzon will be with her and protect her always. Like a lantern in the dark, like a strong guide and porter on a treacherous mountain path, the Gohonzon will guard and protect you, Nichinyo, wherever you go" (WND-1, 832).

My wife and I are earnestly chanting Nam-myoho-renge-kyo for all the Buddhas, bodhisattvas and heavenly deities—the positive forces in the universe—to resolutely protect not only the dedicated mothers of kosen-rufu, but also all our cherished members in Amami.

Mr. Tanano: President Ikeda, you once composed the following poem for the Amami members:

> *Be absolutely triumphant*
> *in this lifetime,*
> *knowing your present struggle in Amami*
> *will bring prosperity*
> *to future generations.*

We, of the young men's division, are determined to unite in spirit with the courageous members in Kagoshima Prefecture, Kyushu Region, sending prayers to the Amami members and assisting them in every way possible.

Ms. Kumazawa: At the recent Soka Gakkai Headquarters leaders meeting (held on October 16, 2010), two block[1] leaders shared their experiences—one of whom was from Yakushima Island, also in Kagoshima Prefecture, and the other from your hometown, President Ikeda, Tokyo's Ota Ward. We were all deeply inspired by their reports.

President Ikeda: It is such admirable members who protect, support and expand the Soka Gakkai. The Daishonin would surely shower them with praise.

In a letter to Abutsu-bo, a lay follower on Sado Island, the Daishonin writes, "In the Latter Day of the Law, no treasure tower exists other than the figures of the men and women who embrace the Lotus Sutra [i.e., Nam-myoho-renge-kyo]" (WND-1, 299). The members of the Soka Gakkai who are dedicated to kosen-rufu are themselves supremely dignified treasure towers.

The Family Is the Essential Foundation

Mr. Tanano: The block leaders at that meeting not only recounted their efforts to increase membership on the front lines of our movement and contribute to their local communities, but also their success in showing actual proof of the benefit of their Buddhist practice by creating beautiful and harmonious families.

Every year, the Japanese government conducts a nationwide survey that asks, among other questions, "What is the most important thing in your life?" In recent years, about half of the respondents have answered, "My family"—a fivefold increase compared to fifty years ago.

President Ikeda: The family is the starting point and essential foundation to which we must always return.

There are some families who live in gorgeous mansions and seem to enjoy all the luxuries of life, but whose family members are divided and miserable. In contrast, there are other families who live in small houses but are genuinely happy, because of the friendly and warmhearted ties among family members. No matter what kind of obstacles they may face, they are able to encourage one another, unite together and build a citadel of victory.

One of the three eternal guidelines second Soka Gakkai president Josei Toda left us is "Faith for a harmonious family."[2]

Ms. Kumazawa: These days, we often hear tragic stories on the news that can be traced back to disputes and problems within the family.

President Ikeda: The French historian Jules Michelet (1798–1874) keenly observed, "When the home is shaken, everything is shaken."[3] Even if we talk about peace and happiness, if we ignore the family, it will only be empty words.

The Soka Gakkai has continued to focus on the real-life challenges of the "human revolution" of each individual and the "family revolution" of each family. These efforts may be arduous and painstaking, but they are precisely why our membership is this solid and unshakable.

Ms. Kumazawa: If I may share a little about my own family, my father started practicing Nichiren Buddhism when he was twenty-one, and he received training as a young men's division member in his local organization. My mother joined the Soka Gakkai soon after she married my father, and she gradually learned about faith in Nichiren Buddhism through the support of women's division members. She says that their warm encouragement really helped her grow as a person. Our family is truly grateful to the Soka Gakkai.

President Ikeda: I'm sure your local members are joyfully watching over you in your endeavors, too. This is the warmth of the Soka family.

The Great Teacher Dengyo of Japan states, "But when in the family honor is paid diligently to the teachings [of the Lotus Sutra], the seven disasters will most certainly be banished" (WND-2, 1026). How important it is therefore that the sound of chanting Nam-myoho-renge-kyo comes to resound in more and more homes, and the philosophy of the sanctity of life becomes more widely established in our communities.

Where there is a network of people who encourage, protect and support one another, safe havens of hope that are undefeated by disasters will spread throughout society. And this will lead to the construction of a peaceful and prosperous society based on the life-affirming principles of Buddhism, and firmly grounded in the family and the community.

It's Important To Show Gratitude to Our Parents

Mr. Tanano: There are some young men's division members who are struggling with family problems in the form of parents or wives who oppose or don't support their practice. Nonetheless, they are all striving with the wish that their family will one day practice Nichiren Buddhism.

President Ikeda: There's no need to be impatient or in a hurry. When I first joined the Soka Gakkai, my father disapproved of my practice. I remember my mother went through great pains to mediate between us.

The Daishonin writes: "When ordinary people in the latter age hear this doctrine [of the Lotus Sutra], not only will they themselves attain Buddhahood, but also their fathers and mothers will attain Buddhahood in their present forms. This is the highest expression of filial devotion" (WND-2, 744).

It's important to start with your own human revolution and make your inner Buddhahood shine forth. It's also vital to cherish your family. By showing that you have grown, you will reassure your parents. The Daishonin states: "Nothing is more certain than actual proof" (WND-1, 478), and "Even more valuable than reason and documentary proof is the proof of actual fact" (WND-1, 599).

Mr. Tanano: Often our family members know our true character better than anyone else. Even if we pretend to be someone different, they'll most likely see through it.

Ms. Kumazawa: Not only in Japan, but also in countries around the world, there are many youth division members who, through the example of their growth and development based on faith, inspire other family members to begin practicing Nichiren Buddhism.

President Ikeda: If you change, then your family will also change. Everything begins with you. If you chant earnestly for your family's happiness, your sincerity will reach them without fail.

In a well-known piece of guidance he wrote for the youth, my mentor, second Soka Gakkai president Josei Toda, declared: "Many youth seem not to love even their parents. How, then, can they possibly hope to love others? The effort to overcome the coldness and indifference in our own lives, and attain the same state of compassion as the Buddha is the essence of human revolution."[4]

I hope that all of you, the youth division members, will be good sons and daughters to your parents. There are many things you can do for them that don't require having a lot of money. For instance, you can give them a bright smile, a simple thank-you or just a phone call to see how they're doing. That alone can make parents feel happy and loved.

Family members are connected by profound and wondrous ties. Through the care and appreciation you show them with even simple words or gestures, you can compose an uplifting song of the joy of living and paint a rich canvas of life. You can create a melody that brings happiness to the entire family.

In a letter to a youthful follower Nanjo Tokimitsu, the Daishonin writes: "If the eight-year-old dragon king's daughter can become a Buddha, then what reason is there to believe that our mothers, through the power of this [Lotus] sutra, cannot become Buddhas? Therefore a person who upholds the Lotus Sutra is repaying the debt of gratitude owed to father and mother" (WND-2, 638).

Through the power of the Mystic Law, you can definitely lead your parents who are not practicing Nichiren Buddhism to enlightenment. Please be confident that spending the days of your youth practicing Nichiren Buddhism and sharing it with others is itself the foremost way to repay your debt of gratitude to your parents.

Don't Be Swayed by Devilish Functions

Mr. Tanano: The Ikegami brothers, two faithful followers of the Daishonin, were strongly opposed in their practice by their father. However, they firmly upheld Nichiren Buddhism, and ultimately achieved a harmonious family united in faith.

President Ikeda: Encouraging the Ikegami brothers when they were faced with obstacles, the Daishonin writes: "The devil king of the sixth heaven takes possession of the bodies of wives and children, and causes them to lead their husbands or parents astray. He also possesses the sovereign in order to threaten the votary of the Lotus Sutra, or possesses fathers and mothers, and makes them reproach their filially devoted children" (WND-1, 496).

The workings of the devil king of the sixth heaven aim to prevent people from becoming happy and attaining Buddhahood. They also manifest in actions on the part of those in positions of power or influence to oppress the teacher and disciples who are striving to propagate the correct teaching of Buddhism.

If we discard our faith because of such negative forces, we will not be able to attain Buddhahood in this lifetime. And on a larger scale, the flow of kosen-rufu will be severed. That's why we must not be swayed by devilish functions but have the strength and wisdom to recognize them for what they are.

At times, this negativity may take hold of our parents, spouse or other family members, causing them to attack what's most dear to us or play on our weaknesses. This, however, does not mean that our family members are literally "devils." After all, what we call "devils" are the negative functions inherent in life. Our family itself is an invaluable treasure.

By regarding the challenges we face within our family as a test of our faith, and then summoning forth courage, chanting Nam-myoho-renge-kyo and expanding our life state, we will undoubtedly come to realize that each person in our family is a "good friend," or positive influence, in our lives. This is the power of the Mystic Law. Nichiren Buddhism is a philosophy that enables us to broadly embrace all difficulties in life and move everything in a positive direction.

Ms. Kumazawa: The Ikegami brothers strove just as the Daishonin instructed them and, as a result, their father also came to accept faith in the correct teaching of Nichiren Buddhism.

President Ikeda: It was a victory of the shared commitment of teacher and disciple. The solid unity of the brothers, who faithfully based themselves on the Daishonin's guidance, was what made this achievement possible.

It is sometimes the case that those to whom we are closest take longer than others to understand Nichiren Buddhism. Even if this may be so, we just have to consider it an opportunity to strengthen and forge our faith. We also don't need to rigidly think that we cannot create a harmonious family unless everyone in the family practices Nichiren Buddhism.

There are many parents who do not practice but selflessly work for their children and family who do. Many of our members have nonpracticing family members who encourage and support them in their Soka Gakkai activities. Isn't this already something remarkable? Such people are the embodiment of "heavenly deities," the protective functions of the universe. They deserve our utmost gratitude.

You Can Definitely Transform Your Karma

Ms. Kumazawa: I have some friends who are struggling with violence in the family and conflicts between parents. There are also other members in the young women's division who have faced similar problems.

President Ikeda: I hope you will carefully listen to each person's situation and encourage him or her sincerely and wholeheartedly. You may also want to consult a more experienced women's division member for advice, while taking utmost care to maintain confidentiality.

In a letter to the lay nun Ueno, the mother of Nanjo Tokimitsu, the Daishonin writes, "One who embraces the Lotus Sutra will realize that hell is itself the Land of Tranquil Light" (WND-1, 456).

There are all sorts of family problems that people face. However, SGI members throughout the world have surmounted even the most serious karma and become genuinely happy. This is actual proof of the benefit of practicing Nichiren Buddhism, which members of the Soka Gakkai have consistently demonstrated for the past eighty years.

Mr. Tanano: The other day, I heard a story related to your visit to the Soka Gakkai's training center in Kagoshima, twenty years ago (in September 1990). It was during a typhoon, and you encouraged a youth who was serving there as an event staff.

The youth told you about his early background, including being adopted as a child. In response, you shared with him an episode from *The Heike Story*, a historical novel by the famous Japanese writer Eiji Yoshikawa (1892–1962). In it, an old caretaker says to the young Taira no Kiyomori,[5] who is agonizing over not knowing who his real father is: "Whoever you are [whatever the origins of your birth], you are a man, after all. Take courage . . . Think of the heavens and the earth as your mother—your father."[6]

You then encouraged the young man, saying: "Grow into a strong, fine individual! If you do that, you'll be able to lead both your adoptive parents and your birth parents toward attaining Buddhahood."

President Ikeda: There is no self-pity or weak sentimentalism in Nichiren Buddhism. In whatever circumstance we may be born, we can bring the sun of time without beginning to shine in our lives and go on to proudly fulfill our missions in this lifetime.

Mr. Tanano: That young man is now active on the world stage, carrying out important responsibilities all around the globe. I've heard that his parents are also doing very well.

President Ikeda: That's wonderful. I'm really happy to hear that.

The Daishonin writes, "Because you have read the entirety of the Lotus Sutra with both the physical and spiritual aspects of your life, you will also be able to save your father and mother, your six kinds of relatives [i.e., all of your immediate family], and all living beings" (WND-1, 204).

If one person in the family stands up with an earnest commitment to faith, then all their family members will share in the boundless benefit of the Mystic Law. It is the same as the sun illuminating all things when it rises in the sky.

Ms. Kumazawa: In the young women's division, too, there are many members who have been able to bring harmony to their families and are now vibrantly advancing in their lives.

President Ikeda: If there is even just one person with sincere faith, the entire family will come to be happy and harmonious without fail. The more you have faced hardships in the family, the more you will develop a life state in which you can support and encourage others.

I especially hope our young women will lay the foundation for their happiness and Buddhist practice during their days of youth.

I call on all of you to move forward with patience, wisdom and cheerfulness, in the way most true to yourselves. By doing so, you will open the path of eternal good fortune, benefit and prosperity for all your family and loved ones.

In a sense, we are all Nichiren Daishonin's children. The Soka Gakkai, directly inheriting the Daishonin's spirit, is a family connected by the Mystic Law, practicing in accord with the Buddha's intent and decree. Today, this Soka family has grown to encompass 192 countries and territories, and it is a treasure of humankind.

Shakyamuni's Buddhist Order was called an "invincible" gathering.[7] I hope that you, the youth division members, will joyously and energetically make the "invincible" and ever-victorious gathering of Soka shine even more brilliantly with your passion and strength.

Give Full Play to Your Potential and Build a Youthful Soka Gakkai

Mr. Tanano: We of the young men's division are determined to expand our network, achieving fresh dynamic development and fostering many new capable people.

The Soka Gakkai Study Department Entrance Examination is now just a month away [scheduled to be held on November 28, 2010]. In preparation, youth division members around Japan are energetically studying Nichiren Buddhism.

President Ikeda: Though we speak of the dynamic development of capable people, the basis for this is each person exerting oneself in the two ways of practice and study, while polishing one's faith. While striving to broaden our noble alliance of good among your own generation, it's also important to courageously challenge and develop yourselves.

The Daishonin writes, "My wish is that my disciples will be cubs of the lion king, never to be laughed at by the pack of foxes" (WND-2, 1062). In order to be cubs of the lion king, I hope you will all make earnest efforts to study Nichiren Buddhism.

I want to praise everyone who is preparing for the upcoming entrance examination, despite being busy with work and many other commitments.

I'm sure this experience will become a lifelong treasure. To the seniors in faith who are encouraging and studying together with the exam candidates, I ask that you will do your utmost to support and assist them.

November 18 (2010), our glorious eightieth anniversary, will soon arrive. I am eagerly waiting and wholeheartedly praying for all of you, my friends in the youth division, to give full play to your innate strength and potential as Bodhisattvas of the Earth, and build a new youthful Soka Gakkai for the twenty-first century.

Notes:

1. In Japan and a number of other countries, such as Brazil, the block is the smallest unit of the organization. In many other countries, it corresponds to the group organization.

2. Second Soka Gakkai president Josei Toda laid down the first three guidelines in December 1957, the month in which the Soka Gakkai reached its historic membership goal of 750,000 households, which translates to roughly two million individual members. The first three guidelines are:

- Faith for a harmonious family
- Faith for each person to become happy
- Faith for surmounting obstacles

Of these, President Ikeda writes: "Since that time, we have advanced toward kosen-rufu with these points engraved in our hearts as the three eternal guidelines of the Soka Gakkai. Their purpose is to provide a clear direction or focus, so that members—in their respective circumstances and lives, in their homes, workplaces and communities—will neither be defeated by difficulties nor fall into the trap of negativity and complaint but instead will live with hope and triumph over all" (January 30, 2004, *World Tribune*, p. 1). In December 2003, he added two more guidelines:

- Faith for health and long life
- Faith for absolute victory

3. Translated from French. Jules Michelet, *Histoire de France* (History of France) (Paris: A. Lacroix & Cie Editeurs, 1880), vol. 10, p. 103.

4. Translated from Japanese. Josei Toda, *Toda Josei zenshu* (The Collected Writings of Josei Toda) (Tokyo: Seikyo Shimbunsha, 1981), vol. 1, p. 60.

5. Taira no Kiyomori (1118–81): Leader of the Taira, or Heike, clan. After achieving political preeminence, he dominated the imperial court. He married his daughter to the emperor and eventually installed his grandson on the imperial throne.

6. Eiji Yoshikawa, *The Heike Story,* translated by Fuki Wooyenaka Uramatsu (Rutland, Vermont: Charles E. Tuttle Company, 1956), p. 26.

7. See *The Book of the Kindred Sayings (Sanyutta-Nikāya) or Grouped Suttas, Part 1, Kindred Sayings with Verses (Sagāthā-Vagga),* translated by Mrs. Rhys Davids (Oxford: Pali Text Society, 1993), p. 37.

——— Seventeen ———

The Honor of Making Unseen Efforts for Kosen-rufu, Part 1

Soka Gakkai Young Men's Leader Nobuhisa Tanano: President Ikeda, thank you for starting to write the latest chapter of *The New Human Revolution*, "Protecting the Citadels of Soka."[1] Just as you are teaching us in this chapter, we of the youth division are determined to staunchly protect the Soka Gakkai and further expand our movement for kosen-rufu.

SGI President Ikeda: I'm counting on you, the youth. All of you in the youth division right now will shoulder the future of the Soka Gakkai. I hope you will make unshakable faith and *The Writings of Nichiren Daishonin* your foundations.

During my youth, striving alongside second Soka Gakkai president Josei Toda, I read *The Writings of Nichiren Daishonin* every day with the resolve to engrave each word and sentence in my heart. Among the passages I copied into my diary at the time were the Daishonin's words: "A sword is useless in the hands of a coward. The mighty sword of the Lotus Sutra must be wielded by one courageous in faith. Then one will be as strong as a demon armed with an iron staff" (WND-1, 412). The Soka Gakkai has always triumphed because it has advanced valiantly in accord with this passage.

There is no more wonderful, fulfilling or glorious stage of activity in youth than the great stage of worldwide kosen-rufu. Please strive to your fullest and create a lasting record of achievement.

Soka Gakkai Young Women's Leader Yumiko Kumazawa:
Yes, we will do our best!

Through the Study Department Entrance Examination held last month (on November 28, 2010), many new members challenged themselves in the two ways of practice and study, and grew in faith. Also, in the second half of this year (2010), the youth division members created a dynamic groundswell of Buddhist dialogue that spread throughout Japan, leading many people to join the Soka Gakkai.

We of the young women's division, taking utmost pride in being Ikeda Kayo-kai members, will continue moving forward more cheerfully than ever, with the sun shining in our hearts.

President Ikeda: I'm very happy to hear that.

Every day, I receive letters from all around the world reporting on how new members, Bodhisattvas of the Earth, are emerging. Our youth everywhere are growing splendidly. Indeed, the time has come for the youth to take the lead.

The Soka Gakkai Has Fostered Vast Numbers of Capable People

Mr. Tanano: Thank you for your trust in us.

There are always many guests who attend the satellite broadcasts of the nationwide youth division leaders meetings (often held in conjunction with the Soka Gakkai Headquarters Leaders Meetings). For the majority of them, it's their first time to visit a Soka Gakkai community center.

Even guests who say they initially felt hesitant to enter the center share that they were put at ease after being warmly greeted by the bright smiles of the members of the Soka Group, Gajokai and Byakuren [behind-the-scenes youth training and support groups]. Other guests also mention being favorably impressed by the friendly and welcoming members, and the large number of young people in attendance.

President Ikeda: Having others experience an actual Soka Gakkai meeting is far more effective than the most detailed explanation of the greatness of our organization.

The Daishonin writes, "When one who is able to show clearly visible proof in the present expounds the Lotus Sutra, there also will be persons who will believe" (WND-1, 512). Buddhism is not about abstract theory or empty ideals. It's about demonstrating clear proof in our own lives and embodying the teachings in our behavior as human beings.

Our courageous young men's division members taking initiative to help and serve others; our young women's division members imparting hope to others with vibrant voices—these, too, are actual proof of correct faith and the embodiment of noble actions of Buddhas.

Many thinkers and scholars find the true significance of the Soka Gakkai's educative power in the fact that it has raised countless such young humanistic leaders.

Ms. Kumazawa: After participating in a Soka Gakkai event in Hokkaido,[2] Hakodate University Professor Emeritus Hakushi Kawamura said he was very impressed by our courteous, friendly event staff.

He remarked, "As a university professor, I felt curious as to how the Soka Gakkai could foster such fine young people."

And he went on to say, "I believe that the Soka Gakkai—a peace movement built through the mentor-disciple relationship of its first three presidents—is one of the few religious organizations in Japan today that can inspire and motivate the youth."[3]

I'm sure these words will also be a great source of encouragement to the Hokkaido members, who are currently braving winter blizzards and difficult economic times.

President Ikeda: Perceptive leaders are seriously thinking about how to raise the youth, the pillar of our future, and taking action toward that end. That's why they have a deep understanding of the significance of the Soka Gakkai's efforts to educate and empower ordinary people and cultivate humanistic values—efforts that have produced vast numbers of capable individuals who are positively contributing to society.

The event staff who greet those arriving at our facilities are the face of the Soka Gakkai. Top business executives and educators, who personally know how hard it is to foster people, are discerning judges of character. The reception they get from our youth, even down to the manner in which they greet them, tells them a great deal.

Respect Everyone as Buddhas

Mr. Tanano: Last month (in November 2010), a Chubu Region[4] women's division member invited a friend to attend a meeting at a Soka Gakkai community center. During the meeting, her friend fell ill, and the Soka Group, Gajokai and nurses group members assisted her with great care and kindness. Deeply moved by their considerate response, she decided to join the Soka Gakkai this month.

Ms. Kumazawa: The guests who come to our meetings, especially those of our own generation, are always surprised and impressed when they are told that the staff protecting our centers and supporting our meetings are all volunteers.

President Ikeda: These are difficult economic times, and social ties in our communities in Japan have also grown strained and distant. Many people have their hands full just dealing with their own problems and situations.

Nevertheless, our members are exerting themselves selflessly for the welfare of others, for their communities and for kosen-rufu even when their own situations may be challenging. There is no more noble work of the Buddha than this.

The Record of the Orally Transmitted Teachings states: "The Buddha preached the Lotus Sutra over a period of eight years, and eight characters sum up the message that he has left behind for living beings in this later age, the Latter Day of the Law. It is [the eight characters that make up the passage, which reads:] ". . . you should rise and greet [others] from afar, showing [them] the same respect you would a Buddha" (p. 192).

Mr. Tanano: The Daishonin is saying here that this passage about showing others the same respect we would a Buddha captures the essence of the entire twenty-eight chapters of the Lotus Sutra, isn't he?

President Ikeda: Yes, that's correct.

There are days when the cold winter winds blow, when the hot summer sun is beating down, when it's pouring rain or when heavy snow is falling. But no matter what challenges our young men and women of the Soka Group, Gajokai and Byakuren face, they always greet those arriving at our facilities with the respect befitting Buddhas, just as the passage from the Lotus Sutra states.

They are carrying out their duties with a spirit of venerating and serving everyone as Buddhas. There is nothing more praiseworthy. Through their behavior, they are putting into practice the passage. "You should rise and greet [others] from afar, showing [them] the same respect you would a Buddha," which is "the foremost point [the Buddha] wished to convey to us" (see OTT, 192).

Our behind-the-scenes group members are serving our members, who are the emissaries of the Buddha, and resolutely protecting the harmonious gathering of the Soka Gakkai, the sole organization advancing kosen-rufu in the present age.

The Daishonin writes, "The blessings to be obtained [by praising and making offerings to the votary of the Lotus Sutra in this latter age] . . .

are a hundred, thousand, ten thousand, million times greater than those to be obtained by conducting oneself with a believing heart in the three categories of body, mouth, and mind, and offering alms to the living body of the Buddha for an entire kalpa" (WND-1, 510).

By devoting yourself for the sake of your fellow members, you are all accumulating immeasurable and boundless benefit and good fortune. Your unseen efforts for kosen-rufu will surely activate the positive forces throughout the universe to reward and protect you in accord with the workings of cause and effect.

I'd like to take this opportunity to once again convey my heartfelt gratitude to all the members of the Soka Group, Gajokai and Byakuren for protecting and supporting our citadels of kosen-rufu, as well as to everyone who is making outstanding contributions to our movement far from the limelight. I'm wholeheartedly chanting for the health, safety and well-being of all of you.

Mr. Tanano: Thank you very much. The youth will continue to carry out their missions striving behind the scenes for kosen-rufu with pride and honor.

The Sincere and Earnest Will Win in the End

President Ikeda: Nichiren writes: "The Buddha taught that one, from the very moment of one's birth, is accompanied by two messengers, Same Birth and Same Name, who are sent by heaven and who follow one as closely as one's own shadow, never parting from one even for an instant. These two take turns ascending to heaven to report one's offenses and good deeds, both great and small, without overlooking the slightest detail" (WND-1, 316).

The Buddhas and bodhisattvas throughout the universe are aware of all the noble unseen efforts you are making to chant for others and support your fellow members, and of how much thought and care you are putting into fulfilling your responsibilities. By the same token, they also know when you are neglecting your duties, thinking that no one will notice. This is merely another way of expressing the law of cause and effect, the workings of which are inescapable.

How seriously we pray and exert ourselves are all engraved in our lives. Those who practice sincerely and earnestly will definitely win in the end. They will accrue immense benefit and good fortune without fail. This is the conclusion I have reached from upholding faith in the Mystic Law for more than sixty years.

The Daishonin writes: "Where there is unseen virtue, there will be visible reward" (WND-1, 907); and "Though one's trustworthiness may at first go unnoticed, in time it will be openly rewarded" (WND-2, 636).

Ms. Kumazawa: President Ikeda, you and Mrs. Ikeda have shown through your own lives the truth of these passages.

President Ikeda: All the actions we take for kosen-rufu will become a cause toward attaining Buddhahood and enable us to reveal our Buddha nature. And by revealing our Buddha nature, the "heavenly deities"—the positive functions of the universe—will assist and protect us. As Nichiren writes, we will surely gain "visible reward" and be "openly rewarded."

Buddhism does not exist somewhere apart from reality. Therefore, the efforts you make for the sake of kosen-rufu will all become your own benefit. And they will also become a cause that will lead your family and loved ones to enjoy great benefit in lifetime after lifetime. Whether or not your efforts may be recognized by others, please be assured that you will most certainly be rewarded by the workings of the Mystic Law.

Herbie Hancock, a world-renowned jazz musician and SGI-USA member, has also willingly served behind the scenes to support various SGI activities.

I heard that when Japanese newspaper reporters once saw this, they were astonished that such a famous musician was working so hard as an ordinary event staff.

Mr. Tanano: You have led the way, President Ikeda, in exemplifying this spirit. In your youthful diary, you write: "In any general meeting, or any important campaign, I am always striving behind the scenes, unknown to anyone, without worrying whether anyone appreciates me . . . there I pour my entire life into leading the struggle and ensuring the success of the events. I smile happily at this destiny. I firmly believe that everything is revealed under the light of the Mystic Law."[5]

Let's Respond to Our Mentor

President Ikeda: Even if no one appreciated or praised me, or if they instead criticized or spoke ill of me, I was still determined to carry out my mission with a smile. All I cared for was to respond to my mentor and strive for kosen-rufu. That was how I spent my youth.

In a letter to Nichigen-nyo, the wife of Shijo Kingo, the Daishonin writes: "Let others hate you if they will. What have you to complain of, if you are cherished by Shakyamuni Buddha, Many Treasures Buddha, and the Buddhas of the ten directions, as well as by [the heavenly deities] Brahma, Shakra, and the gods of the sun and moon? As long as you are praised by the Lotus Sutra, what cause have you for discontent?" (WND-1, 464).

Working at Mr. Toda's side, I always gave my all to planning and organizing meetings and events. I made sure that we had enough event staff, took measures in case of rain, arranged cars and trains for transportation, and did everything I could to ensure that the participants would enjoy the meeting and return home filled with fresh determination. I prayed with all my might and exerted "millions of kalpas of effort" (see OTT, 214). My wife was just as committed and chanted just as earnestly.

Because I strove tirelessly in my youth, I fully understand the feelings of the youth division members and everyone else making efforts behind the scenes.

I can relate to their problems and difficulties as if they were my own. This is also why I've continuously focused on encouraging those working out of the limelight. And they have responded to my encouragement. Because of this, the Soka Gakkai has grown into the global organization it is today.

Ms. Kumazawa: President Ikeda, we of the young women's division are determined to faithfully inherit and carry on the spirit shared by you and Mrs. Ikeda.

President Ikeda: Mr. Toda once said, "Only by earnestly challenging yourself amid a difficult situation can you attain true greatness as a human being."

Adversity builds character. On the solid foundation you forge through experiencing hardships, magnificent flowers of victory in life will eventually bloom.

Notes:

1. In this chapter (vol. 24, chapter 2), SGI President Ikeda writes about the behind-the-scenes groups—especially, the Byakuren Group, the Soka Group and the Gajokai.

2. Hokkaido is the northernmost of Japan's four main islands.

3. Translated from Japanese. *Intabyu—Soto kara mita Soka Gakkai* (Interviews: Impressions on the Soka Gakkai Seen from the Outside), edited by Daisanbunmei Henshu-bu (The Editorial Staff of Daisanbunmei) (Tokyo: Daisanbunmei-sha, 2008), vol. 2, pp. 84, 86.

4. In the Soka Gakkai organization, Chubu Region encompasses Aichi, Mie and Gifu prefectures.

5. See Daisaku Ikeda, *A Youthful Diary: One Man's Journey from the Beginning of Faith to Worldwide Leadership for Peace* (Santa Monica, California: World Tribune Press, 2000), p. 315.

——— Eighteen ———

The Honor of Making Unseen Efforts for Kosen-rufu, Part 2

Soka Gakkai Young Women's Leader Yumiko Kumazawa:
All throughout Japan, members of the Byakuren [a young women's behind-the-scenes training and support group] are steadfastly sharing Nichiren Buddhism with their friends. In September (2010), a Byakuren member in Gifu Prefecture roused the courage to invite one of her friends from college to a Soka Gakkai meeting.

Her friend had always wanted to contribute to peace, but had been unable to do so after being deeply hurt when another friend made fun of her dream. However, after attending the Soka Gakkai meeting and learning about our activities to promote peace and culture, she was very moved. She later participated in several other meetings with the Gifu member, including a Byakuren general meeting, and finally said to her, "I also want to dedicate my life to others' happiness." The friend joined the Soka Gakkai on November 12, Young Women's Division Day.[1]

This experience inspired many other members to introduce their friends to Nichiren Buddhism.

SGI President Ikeda: That's wonderful!

All it takes is just one person. If one person rises to action, everyone else will follow suit. Nichiren Daishonin offers this allegory, "The situation is like the joints in a piece of bamboo: if one joint is ruptured, then all the joints will split" (WND-1, 512).

It's not about comparing ourselves with others, but how we are challenging ourselves. We need to summon courage from within and break through our limitations. That's how the vast frontiers of kosen-rufu are opened.

Soka Gakkai Young Men's Leader Nobuhisa Tanano: In the young men's division, too, the members of the Soka Group and Gajokai academies [young men's behind-the-scenes training and support groups] are taking the lead in sharing Nichiren Buddhism with others.

One young men's division member from Osaka joined the Gajokai Academy this year (2010) out of a wish to improve himself as a person. Due to the economic downturn, the company he ran was failing, and he was struggling financially. But, precisely because he was facing obstacles, he resolved to introduce Nichiren Buddhism to his friends. He went as far as Ishikawa Prefecture [on the Japan Sea coast] to talk with a friend about Nichiren Buddhism and, as a result, the friend decided to become a Soka Gakkai member.

Meanwhile, as he tackled his situation while making the word *sincerity* his motto, just as you taught, his business improved significantly. Now, he says that he almost has too much work and busily travels all around Japan.

It's Important To Develop Ourselves Through Training

President Ikeda: When youth division members rally other youth and start advancing together with youthful creativity and a pioneering spirit, they will build fresh networks for kosen-rufu that will pave the way to an age of humanism.

There is no greater joy than propagating the Mystic Law. The benefit and good fortune we gain by wishing for our friends' happiness, earnestly chanting Nam-myoho-renge-kyo for them and telling them about the greatness of Nichiren Buddhism are everlasting.

There are times when even though we exert ourselves in sharing the philosophy of Buddhism with others, they don't start practicing. But that's fine, too, because we have already sown deep in their lives the seeds for attaining Buddhahood. What's important is to have the courage to continue to talk to them with genuine care. By doing that, you yourself above all will benefit from it, vastly expanding your life state and deepening your conviction in Nichiren Buddhism.

Those who have striven wholeheartedly in their youth to introduce others to Nichiren Buddhism are strong. They lay an indestructible foundation for victory in their lives. Now is the best opportunity for all of you, the youth division members, to build this foundation.

Mr. Tanano: Many young men's division leaders say that they have established the basis of their faith during their days of training in the Soka Group or Gajokai academies. They fondly recall how much their seniors in faith had helped and supported them. The seniors in faith would chant with them or listen to their problems and encourage them. They would do this so passionately that they sometimes felt like it was too much.

But the more time passed, the deeper the appreciation they felt for their seniors in faith.

President Ikeda: I'm sure the earnest care shown to these young men may seem a bit of a burden to them at times. But the seniors in faith who are offering their juniors support are also really commendable. I'm sure many of them are busy with their jobs and also struggling with their own personal problems. Still, they squeeze time out of their busy schedules to meet with and encourage their juniors. It is thanks to such seniors in faith who spare no effort for the sake of supporting their juniors that the Soka Gakkai has fostered a steady stream of capable individuals. And thanks to them, kosen-rufu can continue to develop unceasingly into the future.

Ms. Kumazawa: A Japanese human rights activist, who spoke at a lecture organized by the Soka Gakkai and was impressed at the sight of the youth division members energetically assisting behind the scenes with a deep sense of commitment, said that in them, he sees the great significance of the Soka Gakkai's existence. He also voiced his admiration for the high level of training the youth were obviously receiving.

President Ikeda: The Italian Renaissance scholar Leonardo Bruni (circa 1370–1444) stated, "The power of training is in fact great, and great are its effects."[2] Those who receive thorough training during their youth will with time develop the ability to make great new achievements.

The Daishonin writes: "The deeper the roots, the more luxuriant the branches. The farther the source, the longer the stream" (WND-1, 940). In life, too, we must establish solid roots and cultivate a rich source. That's what training in our youth is all about.

The Soka Gakkai is fostering contributive citizens who will build a better society. And it is producing capable individuals, who are embodying the profound life-affirming philosophy of Nichiren Buddhism and playing active roles in all spheres in society.

Mr. Tanano: We of the young men's division will continue to encourage one another and develop ourselves as we engage in Soka Gakkai activities. Especially during the New Year's holiday period, we will make sure to remind members at our local community centers to take every caution to prevent fires and any other accidents.

President Ikeda: Yes, I'm counting on all of you.

We mustn't allow any accidents to happen. Otherwise, the members will suffer. The Daishonin writes, "The protection of the gods depends on the strength of one's faith" (WND-1, 953). And he also warns, "Be even more careful than usual" (WND-2, 731).

Carelessness is absolutely the greatest enemy—I have continued to take leadership with this deep-seated awareness.

I hope all of you will also take full responsibility for protecting the Soka Gakkai, never forgetting to chant Nam-myoho-renge-kyo powerfully and pay careful attention to every detail.

Taking On Challenges Is a Privilege of Youth

Ms. Kumazawa: Today, given Japan's declining birthrate and the rapidly aging population, the numbers of communities with relatively small youth populations are increasing. In the Soka Gakkai, too, there are some areas where our facilities and meetings cannot be staffed by youth alone. What should we do in these kinds of situations?

President Ikeda: That's a very important question.

The basic point is to give careful consideration to each location's individual circumstances. Many new community centers are being built and the types of meetings we hold are also becoming diversified. Often, how things have been done in the past just don't apply anymore. The key is to utilize the wisdom that arises from our care and compassion for our fellow members. I hope everyone will unite together and come up with creative solutions.

While consulting with the men's and women's division members, I ask that you think of ways to ensure that facilities and meetings will run smoothly and the behind-the-scenes group members will not be overburdened.

Fortunately, now we have members of the Ojokai and Kojo-kai (men's division and women's division behind-the-scenes groups, respectively) also on duty at our centers. My wish is that the youth division members will resolutely protect the SGI centers in their local areas, learning from these praiseworthy experienced members, and exchanging ideas and suggestions with them.

Mr. Tanano: Carrying on the noble spirit of staunchly protecting the Soka Gakkai, we, the young men's division members, are determined to further spread the ideals of Nichiren Buddhism and victoriously open a new era.

President Ikeda: First Soka Gakkai president Tsunesaburo Makiguchi declared, "A single lion is worth more than a thousand sheep."

Each of our Soka Gakkai youth division members is a champion more powerful than an army of ten thousand.

Taking on challenges is a privilege of youth. It's crucial for you not to hold back, trying merely to preserve the status quo or avoid making mistakes. Take bold initiative.

If there aren't too many youth division members in your local organization, then you can chant Nam-myoho-renge-kyo so that there will be more. If you think there aren't enough capable individuals there, you can resolve to foster one person into an outstanding leader for kosen-rufu.

The Soka Gakkai started from virtually nothing, and it has now grown to this extent. It was truly an arduous all-out struggle.

The Daishonin writes: "When I, Nichiren, first took faith in the Lotus Sutra, I was like a single drop of water or a single particle of dust in all the country of Japan. But later, when two people, three people, ten people, and eventually a hundred, a thousand, ten thousand, and a million people come to recite the Lotus Sutra and transmit it to others, then they will form a Mount Sumeru of perfect enlightenment, an ocean of great nirvana. Seek no other path by which to attain Buddhahood!" (WND-1, 580). This is the eternal and unchanging formula of kosen-rufu.

All of you, the youth division members, will determine the future course of kosen-rufu and humanity. Please summon your innate power as Bodhisattvas of the Earth and build a new, youthful Soka Gakkai. Next year, the Year of Capable People and Dynamic Development (2011), is an important starting point in which to embark on this undertaking.

The men's and women's division members are also wholeheartedly supporting you in your endeavors. I hope you will challenge yourselves vibrantly as befitting youth and Soka Gakkai members.

Mr. Tanano: Yes, we will do our best!

Next year (2011) will mark twenty years since the Soka Gakkai became independent of the Nichiren Shoshu priesthood (in November 1991) and proudly began walking the great path of Soka Renaissance. In order to be totally victorious in all aspects this upcoming year, we of the young men's division will first make the New Year's meetings a complete success. With the resolve to develop dynamically in 2011, we will greet our fellow members at our local community centers in the highest spirits.

Our Ascent Toward 2030 Begins, Starting With Each of Us

Ms. Kumazawa: Today, there are young women's behind-the-scenes groups like the Byakuren around the world. At SGI culture and community centers everywhere, young women are warmly greeting members and guests with bright smiles.

President Ikeda: We are living in a truly wonderful age. All around the globe, our young men and women, Bodhisattvas of the Earth, are working tirelessly for their communities, societies and for the happiness and peace of humankind. My heart leaps with joy at the thought of how happy this would surely make the Daishonin.

We are now setting out on our great journey toward our one hundredth anniversary (in 2030). Our ascent of this new summit of kosen-rufu will begin—starting here, starting now and starting with each of us.

The year 2030 will also mark the seventieth anniversary of worldwide kosen-rufu.[3]

What a glorious and magnificent age of widespread propagation of the

Mystic Law we are sure to see at that time.

The Daishonin says that the word *emerging* [with regard to multitudes of bodhisattvas "emerging from the earth" (LSOC, 263)] indicates that at the time of kosen-rufu, the Lotus Sutra will come to be practiced widely by people throughout the world (see GZ, 834).[4]

Now, more than ever, the world is seeking the wisdom of the Mystic Law.

I hope you will all share the same dedication in faith with me once again in the year ahead. Please take steady and noble steps forward in accord with the principle that "unseen virtue brings about visible reward" (WND-1, 940).

I am praying for all of you to joyfully and vigorously join together with youth around the world to create a brilliant and astonishing record of successive victories.

Notes:

1. On November 12, 1961, the Soka Gakkai young women's division held a general meeting bringing together eighty-five thousand young women. This date came to be known as Soka Gakkai Young Women's Division Day. The Soka Gakkai also celebrates July 19, the day in 1951 when the young women's division was founded.

2. Translated from Latin. Leonardo Bruni, *Dialogi ad Petrum Paulum Histrum* (Dialogue dedicated to Petrum Paulum Histrum) (Florence: Leo S. Olschki Editore, 1994), p. 251.

3. President Ikeda embarked on his first journey for worldwide kosen-rufu on October 2, 1960, a date now celebrated annually as SGI World Peace Day.

4. "Oko Kikigaki" (The Recorded Lectures); not included in WND, vols. 1 and 2.

Buddhist Terms, Concepts and More

Abutsu-bo: Abutsu-bo Nittoku, a lay follower of Nichiren Daishonin. Nittoku is his Buddhist name, but he was commonly called Abutsu-bo. When Nichiren was exiled to Sado Island, Abutsu-bo visited him at Tsukahara to confront him in debate, but was himself converted. He and his wife, the lay nun Sennichi, earnestly served the Daishonin during his exile, supplying him with food and other necessities for more than two years until he was pardoned and left the island in 1274.

Ashoka (268–32 BCE): Third ruler of the Indian Maurya dynasty and the first king to unify India. He began as a tyrant, but later converted to Buddhism and governed compassionately in accord with the ideals of Buddhism.

Atsuhara Persecution: A series of threats and acts of violence against followers of Nichiren Daishonin in Atsuhara Village, in Fuji District of Suruga Province, starting in around 1275 and continuing until around 1283. In 1279, twenty farmers, all believers, were arrested on false charges. They were interrogated by Hei no Saemon, the deputy chief of the Office of Military and Police Affairs, who demanded that they renounce their faith. However, not one of them yielded. Hei no Saemon eventually had three of them executed.

attaining Buddhism in this lifetime: Also known as the attainment of Buddhahood in this lifetime. By chanting Nam-myoho-renge-kyo to the Gohonzon with faith and striving to carry out practice for oneself and for others, anyone can achieve the state of Buddhahood or enlightenment in this lifetime.

Bodhisattva Never Disparaging: A bodhisattva described in the 20th chapter of the Lotus Sutra. This bodhisattva, Shakyamuni in a previous lifetime, would bow respectfully to the four kinds of believers—monks, nuns, laymen and laywomen—greeting them with the words: "I have profound reverence for you, I would never dare treat you with disparagement or arrogance. Why? Because you will all practice the bodhisattva way and will then be able to attain Buddhahood" (LSOC, 308).

Bodhisattvas of the Earth: "Emerging from the Earth," the 15th chapter of the Lotus Sutra, describes an innumerable host of bodhisattvas who emerge from beneath the earth, led by Superior Practices, Boundless Practices, Pure Practices and Firmly Established Practices. In "Supernatural Powers," the 21st chapter of the sutra, Shakyamuni transfers the essence of the Lotus Sutra to the Bodhisattvas of the Earth, entrusting them with the mission of propagating it after his death, specifically, in the Latter Day of the Law.

Buddhism is manifested in society: Also, "Buddhism equals society." A principle that points to the inseparable relationship between Buddhism and society. It describes the SGI's view, based on the teachings of the Lotus Sutra and Nichiren Buddhism, that Buddhist practitioners have the power and responsibility to transform for the better not only their own lives but their communities and society as a whole. The Lotus Sutra reads, "and the doctrines that they preach . . . will never be contrary to the true aspect." Regarding this passage, T'ien-t'ai commented, "No worldly affairs of life or work are ever contrary to the true reality." In the Lotus Sutra, the Buddha also says of those who practice the sutra's teaching, "If they should expound some text of the secular world or speak on matters of government or occupations that sustain life, they will in all cases conform to the correct Law." And Nichiren Daishonin writes: "When the skies are clear, the ground is illuminated. Similarly, when one knows the Lotus Sutra, one understands the meaning of all worldly affairs." These passages point to an engaged

Buddhism that aims to transform people's lives and society for the better. This contrasts with the view of most established Buddhist schools that reject society as impure and not conducive to Buddhist practice, and that advocate separation from the secular world or even from this life in pursuit of nirvana or a "pure land."

Buddhism of sowing: The Buddhism that plants the seeds of Buddhahood, or the cause for attaining Buddhahood, in people's lives. In Nichiren's teachings, the Buddhism of sowing indicates the Buddhism of Nichiren, in contrast with that of Shakyamuni, which is called the Buddhism of the harvest. The Buddhism of the harvest is that which can lead to enlightenment only those who received the seeds of Buddhahood by practicing the Buddha's teaching in previous lifetimes. In contrast, the Buddhism of sowing implants the seeds of Buddhahood, or Nam-myoho-renge-kyo, in the lives of those who had no connection with the Buddha's teaching in their past existences, that is, the people of the Latter Day of the Law.

Ceremony in the Air: One of the three assemblies described in the Lotus Sutra, in which the entire gathering is suspended in space above the saha world. It extends from "The Emergence of the Treasure Tower," the sutra's 11th chapter, to the "Entrustment," the 22nd chapter. The heart of this ceremony is the revelation of the Buddha's original enlightenment in the remote past and the transfer of the essence of the sutra to the Bodhisattvas of the Earth, led by Bodhisattva Superior Practices.

changing poison into medicine: A Buddhist principle that explains that through the power of the Mystic Law any problem or suffering can be transformed into the greatest happiness and fulfillment in life.

daimoku: The title of the Lotus Sutra. It also means the chanting of Nam-myoho-renge-kyo.

Dengyo (767–822): Also known as Saicho. The founder of the Tendai (T'ien-t'ai) school in Japan. Often referred to as the Great Teacher Dengyo. He refuted the errors of the six schools of Nara—the established Buddhist schools of the day—and dedicated himself to elevating the Lotus Sutra and establishing a Mahayana ordination platform on Mount Hiei.

devil king of the sixth heaven: Also, devil king or heavenly devil. The king of devils, who dwells in the highest or the sixth heaven of the world of desire. He is also named Freely Enjoying Things Conjured by Others, the king who makes free use of the fruits of others' efforts for his own pleasure. Served by innumerable minions, he obstructs Buddhist practice and delights in sapping the life force of other beings. The devil king is a personification of the negative tendency to force others to one's will at any cost.

dragon king's daughter: Also, the dragon girl. The eight-year-old daughter of Sagara, one of the eight great dragon kings said to dwell in a palace at the bottom of the sea. According to "Devadatta," the 12th chapter of the Lotus Sutra, the dragon girl conceives the desire for enlightenment upon hearing Bodhisattva Manjushri preach the Lotus Sutra in the dragon king's palace. She then appears in front of the assembly of the Lotus Sutra and instantaneously attains Buddhahood in her present form. The dragon girl's enlightenment is a model for the enlightenment of women and reveals the power of the Lotus Sutra to enable all people equally to attain Buddhahood just as they are.

earthly desires are enlightenment: Mahayana Buddhist principle based on the view that earthly desires cannot exist independently on their own; therefore one can attain enlightenment without eliminating earthly desires. This is in contrast with the Hinayana view that extinguishing earthly desires is a prerequisite for enlightenment. Mahayana teachings reveal that earthly desires are one with and inseparable from enlightenment.

emerging from the earth: In *The Heritage of the Ultimate Law of Life*, SGI President Ikeda states: "The Lotus Sutra explains that the Bodhisattvas of the Earth are bodhisattvas who have emerged from the world of truth that lies in the lower region beneath the earth. The Great Teacher T'ien-t'ai says this world of truth means 'the depths of the Dharma nature, the ultimate region of the profound source' (*The Record of the Orally Transmitted Teachings*, p. 119), indicating that the Bodhisattvas of the Earth are enlightened to the ultimate truth. Nevertheless, these bodhisattvas persist in carrying out bodhisattva practice—that is, they continually strive in an evil age to transform their own lives and the lives of others with the goal of achieving kosen-rufu. But in terms of their inner enlightenment, they already possess the life state of Buddhahood that is awakened to the Mystic Law" (p. 106).

establishing the correct teaching for the peace of the land: The principle Nichiren Daishonin sets forth in his treatise "On Establishing the Correct Teaching for the Peace of the Land," in which he teaches practitioners the importance of spreading the correct teaching so that all people can enjoy security, peace and advancement.

faith equals daily life: When we apply our Buddhist practice to the issues and problems we encounter in daily life, those challenges become stimuli—causes or conditions—that enable us to bring forth and manifest Buddhahood. Our daily lives become the stage upon which we carry out a drama of deep internal life reformation.

five impurities: Impurity of the age, of desire, of living beings, of thought (or view) and of life span. The "Expedient Means" (second) chapter of the Lotus Sutra says: "The Buddhas appear in evil worlds of five impurities . . . In this evil world of the five impurities those who merely delight in and are attached to the desires, living beings such as this in the end will never seek the Buddha way." (1) Impurity of the age includes repeated disruptions of the social or natural environment.

(2) Impurity of desire is the tendency to be ruled by the five delusive inclinations, i.e., greed, anger, foolishness, arrogance and doubt. (3) Impurity of living beings is the physical and spiritual decline of human beings. (4) Impurity of thought, or impurity of view, is the prevalence of wrong views such as the five false views. (5) Impurity of life span is the shortening of the life spans of living beings.

five senior priests: Five of the six senior priests designated by Nichiren Daishonin as his principal disciples, but who betrayed his teachings after his death. Nikko Shonin was the only one among these original six senior disciples to correctly carry on the Daishonin's teachings.

four great bodhisattvas: The four great bodhisattvas are Superior Practices, Boundless Practices, Pure Practices and Firmly Established Practices.

four kinds of believers: Four categories of people who believe in Buddhism—monks (Skt *bhikshu*), nuns (*bhikshuni*), laymen (*upasaka*) and laywomen (*upasika*).

four sufferings: The four universal sufferings: birth, aging, sickness and death. Various sutras describe Shakyamuni's quest for enlightenment as being motivated by a desire to find a solution to these four sufferings.

four virtues: Eternity, happiness, true self and purity. Describing the noble qualities of the Buddha's life, they are explained as follows: "eternity" means unchanging and eternal; "happiness" means tranquillity that transcends all suffering; "true self" means true and intrinsic nature; and "purity" means free of illusion or mistaken conduct.

fundamental darkness: The most deeply rooted illusion inherent in life, said to give rise to all other illusions. The inability to see or recognize the truth, particularly, the true nature of one's life.

good friend: Also, good companion or good teacher. One who leads others to the correct teaching or helps them in their practice of the correct teaching.

heavenly deities: Also known as heavenly gods, benevolent deities, Buddhist gods, protective gods, protective forces, etc. Gods or forces that protect the correct Buddhist teaching and its practitioners. Generally refers to the Buddhist pantheon including Brahma, Shakra, the four heavenly kings, the Sun Goddess, the gods of the sun and moon, and other deities. Many of these gods and deities were traditionally revered in Indian, China and Japan. They became part of Buddhist thought as Buddhism flourished in those areas. Rather than primary objects of belief or devotion, Buddhism tends to view them as functioning to support and protect the Buddha, the Law, or Buddhist teachings, and practitioners.

human revolution: Second Soka Gakkai president Josei Toda used this term to describe the process of attaining Buddhahood, a self-transformation achieved through Nichiren Buddhist practice. This transformation involves breaking the shackles of our ego-centered "lesser selves" and revealing our "greater selves," wherein we experience deep compassion and joyfully take action for the sake of others, and ultimately, all humanity.

Ikegami brothers: Leading disciples of Nichiren Daishonin. The elder brother, Munenaka, was twice disowned by their father, who was a follower of Ryokan, the chief priest of Gokuraku-ji—a temple of the True Word Precepts school—and a person hostile to the Daishonin. At the same time, their father tempted Munenaga, the younger brother, to abandon his faith in the Daishonin's teaching and take his brother's place as the next head of the family. Despite these adversities, the brothers persevered in their Buddhist practice. The father later rescinded Munenaka's disinheritance, and in the end took faith in the Daishonin's teaching.

Izu Exile: One of the four major persecutions of Nichiren Daishonin. The Daishonin was exiled to Ito in Izu Province (part of present-day Shizuoka Prefecture) from May 1261 through February 1263. Banishment of Nichiren by the Kamakura shogunate to Ito in Izu Province, Japan, from the twelfth day of the fifth month, 1261, to the twenty-second day of the second month, 1263. After Nichiren narrowly escaped the attempt on his life at Matsubagayatsu, he fled to his disciple Toki Jonin's house in Shimosa Province. When he reappeared in Kamakura in the spring of 1261 and resumed his propagation activities, the shogunate arrested him and, without due investigation, ordered him exiled to Ito on the Izu Peninsula.

kalpa: In ancient Indian cosmology, an extremely long period of time.

Komatsubara Persecution: One of the four major persecutions of Nichiren Daishonin. An attempt by Tojo Kagenobu and his men to kill Nichiren at Komatsubara in Awa Province, Japan, on the eleventh day of the eleventh month, 1264. Kagenobu, the steward of Tojo Village and a believer of the Pure Land teachings, had tried but failed to harm Nichiren earlier when the latter publicly proclaimed his teaching and denounced the Pure Land teachings in 1253. Nichiren was aided in escaping at that time. After being pardoned from his exile in Izu (1261–1263), Nichiren returned to Kamakura. In 1264 he visited his native village in Awa. His father had already died in 1258, and his mother was now seriously ill. Nichiren prayed for her, and she recovered from her illness, living four more years. Nichiren stayed in Awa for a while, taking lodging at a temple called Renge-ji. At that time, a believer named Kudo Yoshitaka invited Nichiren to stay at his home. At dusk, en route to Yoshitaka's residence, Nichiren and his party of about ten people were ambushed by Kagenobu and his men at a place known as Komatsubara. In the ensuing fight, Nichiren suffered a sword cut to his forehead, and his left hand was broken; among his followers, Kyonin-bo was killed, and Kudo Yoshitaka died of the wounds he sustained.

kosen-rufu: Literally, "to widely declare and spread." Nichiren Daishonin defines Nam-myoho-renge-kyo as the Law to be widely declared and spread throughout the world. Kosen-rufu refers to the process of securing lasting peace and happiness for all humankind by establishing the humanistic ideals of Nichiren Buddhism in society.

Land of Tranquil Light: Also, Land of Eternally Tranquil Light. The Buddha land, which is free from impermanence and impurity. In many sutras, the actual saha world in which human beings dwell is described as an impure land filled with delusions and sufferings, while the Buddha land is described as a pure land free from these and far removed from this saha world. In contrast, the Lotus Sutra reveals the saha world to be the Buddha land, or the Land of Eternally Tranquil Light, and explains that the nature of a land is determined by the minds of its inhabitants.

Latter Day of the Law: One of the three consecutive periods or stages into which the time following Shakyamuni Buddha's death is divided: The Former Day, Middle Day and Latter Day of the Law. The Former Day of the Law is an age after the Buddha's passing when people correctly transmit and practice the Buddha's teaching. The Middle Day is a time when the teaching grows formalized and rigid. The ensuing period, known as the Latter Day, is a time when people lose sight of the correct teaching and when society is rife with confusion and conflict.

many in body, one in mind: A concept used to describe ideal unity. Nichiren Daishonin used the phrase to encourage unity among his followers. This expression can also be translated as "different in body, same in spirit." "Different in body" can be interpreted as suggesting the uniqueness of individuals, and "same in spirit," a goal or commitment shared among individuals.

Matsubagayatsu Persecution: One of the four major persecutions of Nichiren Daishonin. An attempt on Nichiren's life by believers of the Pure Land (Jodo) school at his dwelling at Matsubagayatsu in Kamakura, Japan, on the twenty-seventh day of the eighth month, 1260. The attack was motivated by anger at Nichiren's criticism of Honen, the founder of the Pure Land school, and his teachings. On the night of the attack, a group of several hundred people besieged Nichiren's dwelling at Matsubagayatsu, though he had already managed to escape. He then went to the home of his follower Toki Jonin in Shimosa Province, where he spread his teachings for nearly half a year until he returned to Kamakura the following spring.

Miao-lo (711–82): Also known as Chan-jan and the Great Teacher Miao-lo. A patriarch of the T'ien-t'ai school in China. He is revered as the school's restorer.

mutual possession of the Ten Worlds: The principle that each of the Ten Worlds possesses the potential for all ten within itself. "Mutual possession" means that life is not fixed in one or another of the Ten Worlds, but can manifest any of the ten—from hell to the state of Buddhahood—at any given moment. The important point of this principle is that all beings in any of the nine worlds possess the Buddha nature. This means that every person has the potential to manifest Buddhahood, while a Buddha also possesses the nine worlds and in this sense is not separate or different from ordinary people.

Nanjo Tokimitsu (1259–1332): A staunch followr of Nichiren Daishonin and the steward of Ueno Village in Fuji District of Suruga Province (part of present-day Shizuoka Prefecture). During the Atsuhara Persecution, Tokimitsu used his influence to protect his fellow believers, sheltering some in his home. Nichiren honored him for his courage and tireless efforts by calling him "Ueno the Worthy," though he was only about twenty at the time.

Nichigen-nyo (1242–1303): A lay follower of Nichiren and the wife of Shijo Kingo, a samurai who lived in Kamakura in Japan and served the Ema family of the ruling Hojo clan. Nichigen-nyo is most likely the name Nichiren gave her. Their first daughter, Tsukimaro, and the second, Kyo'o, were named by Nichiren. Nichigen-nyo received several letters from Nichiren. When Shijo Kingo visited Nichiren, who was then in exile on Sado Island, he praised Nichigen-nyo for her faith and her willingness to send her husband to Sado, even though, in such perilous times, she had no one else on whom to rely.

Nichimyo: A lay follower of Nichiren who lived in Kamakura, Japan. Widowed, she traveled alone with her infant daughter, Oto, all the way from Kamakura to visit Nichiren while he was living in exile on Sado Island. In recognition of her pure faith, Nichiren sent a letter to her in Kamakura in the fifth month of 1272, in which he wrote: "You are the foremost votary of the Lotus Sutra among the women of Japan. Therefore, following the example of Bodhisattva Never Disparaging, I bestow on you the Buddhist name Sage Nichimyo."

Nichiren Daishonin: The thirteenth-century Japanese Buddhist teacher and reformer who taught that all people have the potential for enlightenment. On April 28, 1253, at age thirty-two, Nichiren declared the establishment of his teaching at Seicho-ji, a temple in Awa Province, and on October 12, 1279, he established the Gohonzon as the object of devotion. He taught that chanting Nam-myoho-renge-kyo with faith in the Gohonzon is the practice that enables people to attain Buddhahahood. *Daishonin* is an honorific title that means "great sage." Nichiren was born on February 16, 1222, in Tojo Village of Awa Province, Japan, and died on October 13, 1282, at the age of sixty-one.

Nikko Shonin (1246–1333): Nichiren's disciple and the only one of the six senior priests who remained true to Nichiren's spirit. He became

Nichiren's disciple at a young age, serving him devotedly and even accompanying him into exile on Sado Island. When Nichiren returned to Mount Minobu, Nikko devoted his energies to propagating activities in Suruga Province (part of present-day Shizuoka Prefecture) and surrounding areas. After Nichiren's passing, the other senior priests gradually began to distance themselves from their mentor's teachings. As a result, Nikko determined to part ways with them. He settled in Suruga's Fuji District, where he dedicated the rest of his life to protecting and propagating Nichiren's teaching and to raising disciples.

oneness of mentor and disciple: This is a philosophical, as well as a practical concept. Disciples reach the same state of Buddhahood as their mentor by practicing the teachings of the latter. In Nichiren Buddhism, this is the direct way to enlightenment, that is, to believe in the Gohonzon and practice according to the Daishonin's teachings.

purification of the six sense organs: Also, purification of the six senses. The six sense organs or faculties of awareness are the eyes, ears, nose, tongue, body and mind. Their purification means that they function correctly and become pure, free of influence of earthly desires, making it possible to apprehend all things correctly.

refuting the erroneous and revealing the true: The practice of pointing out the error of misleading teachings, beliefs or assumptions that lead to unhappiness in order to help people break their attachments to them, while making clear to them the correct principle or teaching for achieving absolute happiness and enlightenment. This was the basic approach of Nichiren Daishonin in pointing out the errors of the established Buddhist schools of his day and leading people to take faith in and practice the Lotus Sutra, or Mystic Law.

Ryokan (1217–1303): Also known as Ninsho. A priest of the True Word

Precepts school in Japan. With the patronage of the Hojo clan, Ryokan became chief priest of Gokuraku-ji, a temple in Kamakura. He undertook numerous social welfare projects, including building hospitals and roads, and commanded enormous influence both among government officials and the general populace. He was hostile to the Daishonin and actively conspired with the authorities to have him and his followers persecuted. During the great drought of 1271, Ryokan vied with the Daishonin in praying for rain and failed. After that he contrived to have accusations brought against the Daishonin by the Nembutsu priest Gyobin, and also stirred the wives of government officials against the Daishonin.

Sado Exile: After the attempt to execute Nichiren at Tatsunokuchi failed, he was confined for nearly a month in Echi at the residence of Homma Rokuro Saemon, the deputy constable of the island province of Sado. Finally the shogunate ordered Nichiren exiled to the island of Sado. On the tenth day of the tenth month, 1271, Nichiren was taken by Homma's warriors from Echi to Sado. They reached Sado on the twenty-eighth day of the tenth month in winter, and, on the first day of the eleventh month, arrived at Tsukahara. Nichiren's quarters were a dilapidated shrine called Sammai-do in the middle of a graveyard. Exposed to the wind, snow fell in through gaping holes in the roof. Later he was transferred to the residence of the lay priest Ichinosawa at Ichinosawa on Sado. While on Sado, Nichiren won many converts, inscribed the Gohonzon for individual believers, maintained frequent correspondence with his followers on the mainland and wrote a number of treatises. On the eighth day of the third month in 1274, a government official arrived on Sado Island with a pardon. Nichiren left Ichinosawa on the thirteenth day of the third month and returned to Kamakura on the twenty-sixth day of the third month.

seven disasters: Disasters said to be caused by slander of the correct Buddhist teaching. In the Benevolent Kings Sutra, they are (1) extraordinary changes of the sun and moon, (2) extraordinary changes of the stars and planets, (3) fires, (4) unseasonable floods, (5) storms, (6) drought and (7) war, including enemy attacks from without and rebellion from within. The Medicine Master Sutra defines the seven disasters as (1) pestilence, (2) foreign invasion, (3) internal strife, (4) extraordinary changes in the heavens, (5) solar and lunar eclipses, (6) unseasonable storms and (7) drought. The seven disasters are often cited together with the three calamities in Nichiren's works as "the three calamities and seven disasters."

Shariputra: One of Shakyamuni's ten major disciples, who was known as foremost in wisdom for his understanding of the true intent of the Buddha's preaching.

Shijo Kingo (c. 1230–1300): One of Nichiren's leading followers. As a samurai retainer, he served the Ema family, a branch of the ruling Hojo clan. Kingo was well versed in both medicine and the martial arts. He is said to have converted to the Daishonin's teachings around 1256. When Nichiren was taken to Tatsunokuchi to be beheaded in 1271, Shijo Kingo accompanied him, resolved to die by his side.

Tatsunokuchi Persecution: One of the four major persecutions of Nichiren. The priest Ryokan of Gokuraku-ji, a temple in Kamakura, was challenged by Nichiren to a contest praying for rain. But when Ryokan's prayers failed to have an effect, he spread false rumors about Nichiren, using his influence with the wives and widows of high government officials. This led to Nichiren's confrontation with Hei no Saemon, deputy chief of the Office of Military and Police Affairs of the Kamakura shogunate, who on September 12, 1271, arrested the Daishonin and had him taken to Tatsunokuchi on the outskirts of Kamakura, where they tried to execute him under cover of darkness. When the execution attempt failed, he was held in detention at the residence of the deputy constable of Sado, Homma Rokuro Saemon, in Echi (part of present-day Kanagawa Prefecture). After a period of about a month, Nichiren was exiled to

Sado Island, which was tantamount to a death sentence. However, when the Daishonin's predictions of internal strife and foreign invasion were fulfilled, the government issued a pardon in March 1274, and Nichiren returned to Kamakura.

ten demon daughters: The ten female protective deities who appear in "Dharani," the 26th chapter of the Lotus Sutra, as the "daughters of rakshasa demons" or the "ten rakshasa daughters." They vow to the Buddha to guard and protect the sutra's votaries.

ten kinds of troops: Also, the ten kinds of troops of the devil king or the ten armies of the devil king. They represent ten kinds of hindrances. Nagarjuna's *Treatise on the Great Perfection of Wisdom* lists them as (1) greed, (2) care and worry, (3) hunger and thirst, (4) love of pleasure, (5) drowsiness and languor, (6) fear, (7) doubt and regret, (8) anger, (9) preoccupation with wealth and fame and (10) arrogance and contempt for others.

three Buddha bodies: Three kinds of body a Buddha may possess. A concept set forth in Mahayana Buddhism to organize different views of the Buddha appearing in the sutras. They are: (1) The Dharma body, or body of the Law. This is the fundamental truth, or Law, to which a Buddha is enlightened. (2) The reward body, obtained as the reward of completing bodhisattva practices and acquiring the Buddha wisdom. (3) The manifested body, or the physical form that a Buddha assumes in this world in order to lead people to happiness.

three categories of action: Also, three types of action. Activities carried out with one's body, mouth and mind, i.e., deeds, words and thoughts. Buddhism holds that karma, good or evil, is created by these three types of action—mental, verbal and physical. Here "action" is the translation of the Sanskrit *karman*.

three martyrs of Atsuhara: Three brothers—Jinshiro, Yagoro and Yarokuro—who were arrested and beheaded during the Atsuhara Persecution. In 1278, propagation of the Daishonin's teachings was advancing rapidly in the Fuji area under the leadership of Nikko, Nichiren's direct disciple. When three priests of Ryusen-ji, a local Tendai school temple, were converted, the temple's deputy chief priest Gyochi became alarmed and started to conspire with authorities to threaten local believers. On September 21, 1279, twenty farmers, all followers of Nichiren Daishonin, were arrested on false charges of stealing rice. Of these twenty, the three brothers were executed for refusing to renounce their faith.

three obstacles and four devils: Various obstacles and hindrances that impede one's practice of Buddhism. The three obstacles are (1) the obstacle of earthly desires, (2) the obstacle of karma and (3) the obstacle of retribution. The four devils are (1) the hindrance of earthly desires, (2) the hindrance of the five components, (3) the hindrance of death and (4) the hindrance of the devil king.

three poisons of greed, anger and foolishness: The fundamental evils inherent in life that give rise to human suffering. In Nagarjuna's *Treatise on the Great Perfection of Wisdom,* the three poisons are regarded as the source of all illusions and earthly desires. The three poisons are so called because they pollute people's lives and work to prevent them from turning their hearts and minds to goodness.

three powerful enemies: Three types of arrogant people who persecute those who propagate the Lotus Sutra in the evil age after Shakyamuni Buddha's death, described in the twenty-line verse section of "Encouraging Devotion," the 13th chapter of the Lotus Sutra. The Great Teacher Miao-lo of China summarizes them as arrogant lay people, arrogant priests and arrogant false sages.

three thousand realms in a single moment of life: A doctrine developed by the Great Teacher T'ien-t'ai of China based on the Lotus Sutra. The principle that all phenomena are contained within a single moment of life, and that a single moment of life permeates the three thousand realms of existence, or the entire phenomenal world.

T'ien-t'ai (538–97): The founder of the T'ien-t'ai school in China. Commonly referred to as the Great Teacher T'ien-t'ai. His lectures were compiled in such works as *The Profound Meaning of the Lotus Sutra, The Words and Phrases of the Lotus Sutra,* and *Great Concentration and Insight.* He spread the Lotus Sutra in China, and established the doctrine of "three thousand realms in a single moment of life."

voluntarily taking on the appropriate karma: Also known as "voluntarily assuming the appropriate karma." This refers to bodhisattvas who, though qualified to receive the pure rewards of Buddhist practice, relinquish them and vowing to be reborn in an impure world in order to save living beings. They spread the Mystic Law while undergoing the same suffering as those born in the evil world due to karma. This term derives from Miao-lo's interpretation of relevant passages in "The Teacher of the Law," the 10th chapter of the Lotus Sutra.

Index